Fifteen Fortunes

Fifteen Fortunes

AN OCTOGENARIAN REFLECTS ON LIFE AS AN ENTREPRENEUR

Robert C. Elmen

Edited by J D Elmen

ISBN-13: 9781484032893
ISBN-10: 1484032896

Edited by J D Elmen

For Rita, my soul mate

Acknowledgments

—◆—

MORE PEOPLE THAN I CAN name here have contributed to the success of Elmen Enterprises throughout the years, and deserve my gratitude. In particular, I want to recognize my late father, Lloyd Elmen, for his initiative in starting the business in the early 1950s; and my late brother, Jim Elmen, for his steadfast partnership and for the energy he brought to the company. In addition to every talented and dedicated manager and employee, I would like to thank Vance Goldammer and Tom Whalen, who have played key roles in supporting our business efforts over the years.

I started writing this book several years ago on a yellow legal pad. When it became obvious that my chicken-scratch handwriting would make it difficult to get the manuscript into a form easily submitted for publication, I switched to an electric typewriter and the 2-finger typing technique. When the first draft of the book was finally completed, I found someone willing to transcribe the handwritten and typed text into a digital file using a word processor. This is when I realized that my refusal to use a computer for anything other than following my stock portfolio probably slowed the writing process significantly.

For taking on the role of deciphering my handwriting in order to create a digital version of the original text, I thank Tiffny Hagan of Virtual Office Advantage in Sioux Falls. For help in getting this manuscript in good shape and ready to send to the publisher, I thank my daughter Julie, who spent many hours dedicated to this project. For proofreading the final draft and locating photographs to include in the book, I thank my daughter Sarah, the family archivist. For proofreading the manuscript more than once in its earlier stages, and for her unremitting patience and support during the writing process, in particular, and also throughout our 60 plus years of marriage - I thank my wife Rita.

I have heard it said that a friend is someone who knows all about you, and still likes you. I'm grateful to our dear friends and overseas travel partners, Loren and Jean Tschetter - for the laughter, companionship, and the many great meals we've shared over the years.

Nothing happens without sufficient motivation. For being a motivating force as I worked on *Fifteen Fortunes*, I thank my grandchildren: Christopher Ordal, Kjerstin Elmen-Gruys Ackermann, Hanna Elmen-Gruys Setrakian, Erik Ordal, Emily Ordal, Peter Elmen-Gruys, Alex Kopp, Sadie Kopp, and Julia Kopp. Without the added incentive to share my story with you, it might have been tempting to give up before the project was finished.

Table of Contents

CHAPTER 1

The Best Laid Plans

———— ✠ ————

Whether you think you can, or think you can't . . . You're right!

~ HENRY FORD (1863-1947), FOUNDER OF FORD MOTOR COMPANY

AS A SERIOUS-MINDED 20-YEAR-OLD COLLEGE sophomore in 1950, I made the decision not to become a physician. This was clearly a turning point in my young life because, 65 years later, my memory tells me exactly where I was sitting at the time in Old Main Library at Augustana College in Sioux Falls, SD. The fact that I had decent biology grades, but not-so-good chemistry grades, probably had something to do with my misgivings about pursuing medicine as a career. But as a 1950s version of what my grandchildren might call a "nerd", I also worried about retiring as a doctor without a known retirement income return. I must have realized at the time that nothing in this life is certain, but I was also cognizant of the fact that hard work and disciplined habits could produce measurable compounded growth from invested savings.

Thinking about all of this as a young adult in Old Main Library helped to clear up the road ahead for me, and the image of myself pondering the direction my life would take has stayed with me all these years. As a young man who had felt the effects of life during the Great Depression, I know I was very concerned about the security of my financial future. Also, the decision to abandon what had been a long-time goal must have made a distinct impression on me.

Old Main, on the campus of Augustana College, Sioux Falls

As a college sophomore, I was intrigued by the idea of being able to concretely measure an increasing net worth, and I wanted to know how combining imagination with hard work might impact this process. Getting a college education while setting out on that quest was as fulfilling and rewarding as it was challenging. Finding time for both work and study during these years was difficult, but keeping track of my meager savings and initial investments was enjoyable; as each grew in size, I gained confidence about my financial future.

In spite of trying to save all the money I could, it was necessary for me to buy a car (a used 1946 Chrysler New Yorker, with a visor over the windshield) for transportation to and from three part-time jobs, home, and school. While attending Augustana College, I worked at the John Morrell meatpacking plant in the canning department, did yard work, handled cleanup for a construction company, and sold tomatoes grown in a community garden near my home. In addition, many of my friends and I joined the US Naval Reserve and eventually became reserve officer candidates (ROCs). We were paid a stipend and also got all-expenses-paid two-week "cruises" each year to places like Jamaica and the former Naval Station Great Lakes in North Chicago, Illinois. We also had two periods of training in California. These part-time work opportunities all helped to pay for my car - and by living at home, I could also afford to pay college tuition if I used some of my savings.

Fundamental business concepts and strategies can be learned through formal education or independent study – and are beyond the scope of this book, which focuses more heavily on my own journey and what I've learned along the way. In order to provide personal and historical context for my experiences as an entrepreneur, I will talk about my Scandinavian heritage, which has given me a respect for the physical and mental effort expended by my ancestors as they toiled in Sweden, Norway, and – eventually – America. Their resourcefulness, creativity, courage, and desire to acquire skills and knowledge through hard work and specialized training led to opportunities for their descendants in the New World. The value many of my ancestors placed on learning and education has given me a strong desire to be educated and to encourage my children and grandchildren to pursue higher education. Elements of my experience that have enriched my life - especially my family - or informed my business career in some way – such as boy scouting, military service, and outdoor activities like hunting and fishing - are also discussed in this book.

Individual chapters will include my thoughts on a variety of business-related topics - such as risk, luck, entrepreneurship, investing, and philanthropy. This content will draw from, or reflect upon, my business-related experiences during a sixty-two-year time span from July 1, 1950, to December 2012. Throughout this time my financial goal never changed, in spite of difficulties - otherwise known as learning opportunities - along the way; it was always to use imagination and hard work to make my investments grow. As a young man I was more focused on building a life for myself and, later, for my family that was free from financial hardship; as I became older and more financially secure, the focus shifted to building wealth and creating exciting business opportunities. There were times when significant losses had to be taken. When this happened, I was always glad to have diversified interests so the more profitable businesses could be expanded to offset a loss in another project.

The meaning of the term *wealthy* has changed over the years, and can mean very different things depending on where one lives and works, as well as what one values. "It's probably true that being rich is more a state of mind than an explicit level of income or wealth. It's a feeling of having enough money so that money is no longer a worry" (*Robert Samuelson, Newsweek*, July 10 2009). Paul Strassels, a financial writer from Rapid City, South Dakota, asked the question, How Much Money Is Enough? in an Augustana Library Association presentation I attended twenty years ago. At that time, he claimed four million dollars was the amount necessary to set up most people with a life of financial freedom and independence going forward. More recently, a 2013 UBS (United Bank of Switzerland) *Investor Watch Report* on defining wealth indicated that nearly 70% of investors with more than $1 million in investable assets don't think of themselves as wealthy. Instead, most respondents said it would take at least $5 million in personal wealth to consider themselves wealthy.

Since the early 1950s, my investor partners and I have launched a number of business projects, sharing the work, worry, and financial results. All told, the time, money, and energy expended over the past six decades have resulted in roughly fifteen separate but overlapping business success stories. There were also about a dozen major losses (but who's counting) from projects that had to be phased out or discontinued in order to maintain the desired net twenty percent return. We all know that failure is often an important stepping-stone to achieving success. As Henry Ford famously said, "The only real mistake is the one from which we learn nothing." For me, without a doubt, the most painful consequence of an unsuccessful business venture is the realization that others who have invested in the idea have lost money. Fortunately, those who have failed along with me have also shared in the satisfying successes. In many of life's worthwhile endeavors, time, money, hard work, and imagination come into play. In the pursuit of wealth, add to this list luck, ambition, and timing - as well as local, national, and global economic realities.

Over the years, I have tried not to confuse the pursuit of wealth with the pursuit of happiness - and to remember that "the happiness of pursuit" is just as important as "the pursuit of happiness". It goes without saying that the world is a vastly different place than it was when I sat pondering my future in the Augustana College Old Main library. Whether you are at the beginning of your business career, partway through the journey, a seasoned entrepreneur - or perhaps even one of my children or grandchildren - I hope that you will find a gem or two in this book that will inform your own situation and interests.

CHAPTER 2

Roots - The Scandinavian Work Ethic Lives On

—⚹—

We don't inherit the earth from our ancestors;

we borrow it from our children.

~ DAVID BROWER (1912-2000), AMERICAN ENVIRONMENTALIST

ALL OF MY ANCESTORS CAME from forested areas of Sweden and Norway. The lives they led while working the rocky soil in those countries could not have been easy. Throughout my business career I have often thought of the various branches of the family tree and taken inspiration from the work ethic of those who came before me.

SWEDISH ANCESTORS

My paternal great-grandfather, Johan Petterson (1812–1877), and great-grandmother, Lisa Stina Jonsdotter (1816–1874), lived on the Elmberg/ Älmberg family farm outside the city of Jönköping in Småland, a province in southern Sweden covered with shining lakes and dense forests. Jönköping is at the southern tip of Lake Vattern, which today is still known for the excellent quality of its water - requiring very little treatment before being pumped into nearby municipalities for drinking. The Petterson family worked the farm themselves, but could occasionally afford to hire farmhands to help with chores, which included, among other tasks, finding grassy areas in the surrounding forests for the cows to graze on. The family fished on Lake Vattern during the summer months and ice-skated on its frozen surface in the winter. During the coldest months, *Ärtsoppa* (pea soup) was often kept warm on the stove for anyone who was hungry.

I recently learned that Ingvar Kamprad, Swedish business magnate and founder of IKEA (the world's largest furniture retailer), was born about 84 miles/126 kilometers from where my ancestors had farmed near Jönköping. In fact, the "E" and "A" in IKEA stand for *Elmtaryd* and *Agunnaryd* - the Kamprad family farm and the village where Ingvar was born in 1926.

My paternal grandfather, Frank Petterson, the ninth child of Johan and Lisa Stina, was born in 1860. He studied at Uppsala College in Sweden before coming to Moline, Illinois, in 1886, where he married Anna Lovisa Pettersdotter. The couple moved to Sioux Falls, Dakota Territory the following year, where Grandpa worked at the rail yard shoveling coal. He had changed his name from Petterson to *Elmen*, likely taken from the name of the family farm (Elmberg) in Sweden. The provenance of the family farm name is not known, but it makes sense to assume that the name relates to the Elm tree species that populated the forests in southern Sweden during the 18th and 19th centuries. Sweden is still a country dominated by forests, and, according to recent opinion polls, the most popular Swedish outdoor activity is "forest walking" (*The Swedish Forestry Model*, Royal Swedish Academy of Agriculture and Forestry, Stockholm, July 2009). In any case, our Swedish heritage is firmly rooted in the country's farming and forest traditions.

In 1921, Grandpa lost the entire amount of his $5,000 inheritance when all but one bank failed in Sioux Falls, South Dakota. Frank and Anna had 8 children. Their first born, Ernest "Doc" (1888-1969), was a Sioux Falls dentist and married Blanche Lee. They had no children of their own but doted on my siblings and me, and on their other nephews and nieces. Lillian (1890-1932), the oldest daughter, suffered from mental illness at a time when effective treatment was not available; she died in a Yankton, South Dakota, institution in 1935.

The third child born to Frank and Anna was Carl (1893-1921). Carl was killed in an elevator accident in downtown Sioux Falls soon after he came back from serving in WWI (the same year Grandpa lost his inheritance). Agnes (1895-1991) married Carl Carlson, and later married Roy Kinney. While she had no children of her own, Agnes cared for the children of others until she was well into her 90s. George "Pete" (1897-1979) graduated from law school but did not practice law. He married [Mary] Ada Roberts and was Potentate of the El Riad Shrine, and served as a city commissioner, in Sioux Falls. George and Ada were the parents of 3 children. Harold "Huts" (1900-1981) worked for the *Argus Leader* newspaper, and LuElla Mauritz was his life long companion. Dorothy (1909-1993), the youngest girl in the family, married Herman Christensen; together, they had 2 children.

My father Lloyd (1902-1995) graduated with honors from the University of South Dakota School of Business. He ran a concession stand in McKennan Park during the summers between his years at the University. Dad was the first college graduate hired at John Morrell & Company, and worked in the superintendent's office until 1948. He married my mother, Sylva Hellie (1908-1997), in 1929; at that time it was really something for a Swede to marry a Norwegian. They had 3 children, including James "Jim" (1932-2006), Elizabeth "Betty" (b. 1938), me (b. 1930).

My wife, Rita (Hale) Elmen, and I have helped organize three Petterson (now Peterson) - Elmen reunions in South Dakota. A genealogy book was compiled by a dozen of us in a boardroom of our office headquarters in Sioux Falls. It was work that was interesting, fun, and fulfilling. Friendships developed, and additional information was obtained from families we met at the various reunions. Rita also has Scandinavian roots; her mother, Sadie Matilda (Fredine) Hale (1902-1972) was Swedish. Rita's father, Harold Elester Hale (1904-1990) is believed to be a descendant of Edward Fuller, one of the Mayflower pilgrims; the line of descendancy would be through Harold's mother, Elmay Clara (Youngs) Hale (1886-1976). Harold - whom everyone called "Hale" - drove a Tastee Bread truck for 30 years before he and Sadie opened The Highway Market in St. James, Minnesota, which they continued to run into their later years.

NORWEGIAN ANCESTORS

Norway was second only to Ireland in the proportion of its population that immigrated to America. Few areas of Norway contributed as large a percentage of their population to the movement as did Valdres, a province in central Norway where our Norwegian ancestors lived. Present and future generations of Helle/Hellie descendants can be proud of their Norwegian heritage. The Helle farm is one of the oldest farms on record in Norway, having been registered in the 1300s. The farm still lies about 100 miles north of Oslo in Valdres, one of two major valleys in the administrative district of Oppland in Southern Norway. In Valdres the growing seasons were short, cool and sometimes wet, resulting in frequent failures of grain crops. In historical documents the Helle farm in Valdres is listed as supporting 2 horses, 8 cows, 4 calves, 2 pigs, 18 sheep, 3 chickens, and 165 Norwegian blue foxes. The pelts of arctic foxes with a slate blue coloration—an expression of a recessive gene—were especially valuable. The animals' fur turned white or light gray in the winter. The population of arctic foxes is dwindling - due, in part, to climate change leading to less snow cover in which to find camouflage in the winter months.

The main local parish, Hore at Huram, in the township of Vang, is one of twenty-six remaining stave church parishes in Norway today. Inside the church, there are pews for the Helle family located across from each other – one side for female family members and the other for male family members. Gravestones bearing the Helle name can be found in the churchyard, which overlooks Lake Slidrejorden. The original church was built around 1180; in 1820 the church was rebuilt to its present shape. Near the entrance to the churchyard is a memorial stone to Queen Gyda, who was reared in Vang. She is credited with challenging King Harald Haarfagre ("Hairfair") to unite the more than 30 Norwegian kingdoms into one national kingdom. She agreed to marry Harald after he succeeded in bringing all of Norway under one crown in 872 AD (*The Seven Wives of Harald Fairhair: 1st King of All Norway - A Viking Saga, by* Marcia Lee Liaklev, 2013).

My great-great grandfather, Stefan Olsen Kubakke Helle, was a chair-maker in the Valdres village of Vang, an area with high rugged mountains and a few fertile valleys, where farming was, and still is, the main occupation. He came to America for the first time in 1846, returning to Valdres in 1848 to spread the word about opportunities on the other side of the Atlantic Ocean. In 1852 he brought 134 relatives and friends back to America with him, half of whom drowned in what we are told was a deliberate boat-ramming incident on Lake Erie. Sadly, his mother, my great-great-great grandmother, was one of the casualties.

My great grandfather Knut Jogerson Helle (1830–1919) continued the Kubakke Helle chair-making tradition. In the wintertime he brought his carpenter's bench from the barn into the living room, placing it between the bed and the open fire. With the light from the fire he would make wagons, sledges, and many other things, including Kubakke chairs. The rounded chair wood was hand-selected and made to fit the contours of the body. Over three thousand chairs were made over several generations. The chairs in the earlier days ranged in price from five to twenty kroner each. I am proud to own one of the chairs built by my great grandfather. He married first to Marit Gjermundsdotter Hoyme in 1858. Marit died the following year after giving birth to their only child - a daughter, Marit. Knut then married Sigrid Olsdotter Skjefte in 1859 and they were the parents of eight additional children, Marit; Joger; Ole; Knute (my Grandfather); Jorann and Ingeborg (twins); Olaf; and two other girls (both named Marit) who died in infancy.

My grandfather, Knute Knutsson Hellie (1867-1944), said farewell to his parents, the farm, and the Hore Parish community and came to America in 1882 at the age of sixteen; with him were a sister (Mary) and two brothers (Ole K. and Olaf). They settled in Albert Lea, MN, where Knute (now spelled with an "e") began to learn the carpenter's trade; he worked at it for a year before relocating to the village of Hills, Minnesota. The siblings started their journey by boat from Lerdal to Bergen, and then traveled by ship to America. In 1889, grandfather married Sigrid (Sarah) Rovang (1868–1940), whose parents, Gilbert and Anna, owned a farm in Hills, MN, and had previously been in the transportation business in Valdres, Norway.

Sigrid (Sarah) Rovang (1868 - 1940) was born in Big Canoe, Winneshiek County, Iowa and came to the village of Hills in 1871 with her parents, Gilbert and Anna (Westlie) Rovang. From the age of 14, until she was married to Knute in 1891, she made a living as a hired girl with local families. Together, Knute and Sigrid Hellie had 8 children, 7 of whom lived into later adulthood: Clifford (1892-1974), Alma (1894-1959), Geneva Sylva (1896-1898), Grant (1898-1958), Geneva (1901-1988), Esther (1903-1985), Sylva (1908-1997), and Kermit (1911-1963). Geneva Sylva died at age 2; two of the girls born later (Geneva and Sylva, my mother) were namesakes of the older sister they never met. A family reunion was held in August of 2003 for the descendants of Knute and Sigrid Hellie. Those present visited the original home sites and family farms in the Hills, Minnesota, and Sioux Falls, South Dakota, areas.

Knute managed the Tuthill Lumber Company in Hills, Minnesota, beginning in 1905, and the Hills Cement Block and Tile Works beginning in 1908. For 15 years he, along with his cousin, Ole (whose 105th birthday party we attended some years ago), were the leading contractors in the village; during that time, over a hundred residences (several of which are now restored to their original condition) were built. Grandpa Knute and his cousin erected most of the public buildings, including the Hills school and twenty-eight churches, during those years as well. (Grandpa's cousin Ole shouldn't be confused with either of his brothers, Ole K. or Olaf. The name was a common one given to Norwegian males; perhaps the profusion of Ole and Lena Norwegian jokes can be attributed to this fact.)

In addition to the many public and private structures erected by Knute and Ole Helle, a number of the buildings in Hills, including the Christianson Bros. furniture store, were constructed of blocks from the cement plant Knute managed. He also owned, with some debt, a 240-acre farm north of Beaver Creek, Minnesota. Grandpa was on the board of directors of the First National Bank in Hills, and a member of the village council. In 1907, he visited his aged parents, Knut J. and Sigrid O. Helle, in Norway.

Geneva, Esther, Grant, Knute (seated), Sylva (my mother, seated),
Alma, Sigrid (seated), Clifford, and Kermit, 1916

My mother, Sylva Karethe Hellie, was petite, charming, refined, and energetic. Before she married Dad in 1929, she did domestic work at a home on Spring Avenue and 14th Street in Sioux Falls. For a time, she also worked at Fantle's Department Store in downtown Sioux Falls. She lived on South Second and 26th Street when she attended Augustana College and Normal School for a 2-year degree. Mother stayed at home to care for my siblings and me when we were young. She was strict, loving, highly organized, and busy with church activities and bridge games. She also stayed in touch with friends from college days via a "round robin" letter that circulated among them for many years.

Mother didn't have a driver's license until well into her 50s, relying on Dad or others to drive her to appointments and social gatherings. She loved to walk, and never missed a social event due to lack of transportation. In her later years she continued to play a good game of bridge, even after being diagnosed with Alzheimer's. One time when Rita came to pick her up at the retirement center for an outing, Mother got in the car before deciding to go back for a sweater. After waiting 10 or 15 minutes, Rita parked and went in to see what was holding Mother up. She was surprised to find her happily immersed in a game of bridge with friends.

In addition to a keen interest in learning about our family's Norwegian (and Swedish) ancestry, I have a particular fascination with two different elements of Norwegian culture – both related to food and it's preservation. When I travel to Norway, the historical item I most like to look for in the farmland areas is the *stabbur*, a storage shed well known in Scandinavia for its ability to protect food from moisture and rodents. In the high summer pastures of Valdres, it was important to store away the fast-growing hay for the long winter ahead. A wooden shed elevated a few feet off the ground by stone pilings or wood supports at each corner, the stabbur had wood or stone steps leading up to - but set apart from - the shed. Stabburs were typically windowless and had sod roofs that protruded significantly over the exterior walls. They consisted of two separate cube-shaped rooms, which were stacked - with the larger room over the smaller one - like an inverted tower. The lower room was often used to store grain (and/or sometimes livestock), while the upper room was used for harvested vegetables, or to hang meat for smoking.

Jimmy, Mother, Betty, Dad, and me on Christmas Day, 1943

A stabbur could be used to store non-food items as well - household goods, seasonal clothing, or even guests. In Norway, where religion often mixed with superstition in the 1600s and 1700s, intricate woodcarvings of lions, crosses, and other symbols often protected the buildings. In the modern era, stabburs in Norway are sometimes converted to living quarters for tourists and other visitors. One online advertisement for a Norwegian resort called "Stabbursnatt" says, "Would you like to spend the night in one of Norway's typical store/guest houses? Many of them are hundreds of years old! Behind rough sun-darkened log walls, meat used to be salted in big wooden tubs, grain poured into bins, and our beautiful national costumes put into *rosemaled* (painted) chests. In the summer, maids and farmhands sometimes slept there because it was cool and airy. Night mischief was popular!" (www.venturenorway.com/stabbursnatt).

The other thing that fascinates me is the Norwegian cod fishing industry. Bruce Halverson, a friend of mine and former president of Augustana College in Sioux Falls, was aware of my interests in Norwegian history, economic technology, and fishing. He loaned me a book about the history of codfish and the importance of its protein on world development (*Cod, a Biography of the Fish that Changed the World*, by Mark Kurlansky, 1998). The book explains that Basque fishermen had secret cod fishing areas in the late 1400s. They brought salt over to the eastern coast of America and used it to take dried cod back to Norway. Codfish became the major export of Norway before oil from the North Sea. Cod could be dried without salt north of the Arctic Circle. They could be caught almost all year long in Norway. They were an important source of protein that could be taken by ship to other parts of the world.

In 1998, Rita, two of our daughters, and I spent 7 days on the *Hurtigruten* ("fast route") 623-passenger MS Richard With - one of several working ships that travel daily along the 1,500 mile Norwegian coast between Bergen in the south and Kirkenes in the north, delivering freight and passengers to over 30 ports (many of them inaccessible to larger ships) along the way. During the trip along the picturesque fjords and narrow inlets, our daughter, Julie, and I marked my 70th birthday with a day trip to Lofoten, an archipelago known for its dramatic mountains and scenic fishing villages in northern Norway. On the excursion we saw hundreds of wooden racks used for drying cod, and visited an art gallery in Henningsvær where artists portray the beauty and inspiration of the archipelago.

Another enjoyable cod-related experience in Norway took place while our family was on a cruise in Norway to commemorate Rita's and my 50th anniversary in 2002. Several of our grandchildren joined me on a fishing excursion near the North Cape, where we caught over a dozen codfish with the help of an experienced Norwegian fishing boat captain.

Cod fishing with granddaughters Kjerstin and Hanna near the North Cape in Norway, 2002

The pride I have in my Scandinavian heritage has been a source of inspiration for my career in business, and for my life in general. Knowing how hard my Swedish and Norwegian ancestors worked in order to make a good life for themselves and their families has made me want to work hard as well, and to learn all I can in the process.

CHAPTER 3

Teach Your Children Well

—⟋⟋⟍—

Try to learn something about everything, and everything about something.

~ THOMAS HUXLEY (1825-1895), BRITISH BIOLOGIST

THE BAND CROSBY, STILLS, NASH, and Young sings about teaching children according to "a code that you can live by", in their 1970 album *Deja Vu*. Children learn about many things before they go to school. In addition to formal learning, lessons take place when young people observe everything around them. As I look back on the earliest years of my childhood, I realize that I am still able to learn a little something from the memories I took with me from that time.

My family lived in a modest Sioux Falls house, near Emerson School and the park between Sioux Street and South Lake Avenue. Dad's parents lived nearby. Grandpa Frank worked shoveling coal at the railroad nearby. He and Grandma Anna lived on the other side of the railroad tracks on Prospect Street, and had purchased property for house lots to the north of the block. They owned a railcar building that was used for keeping a cow and some chickens. My Dad talked of taking the cow out to look for grass. Milk and eggs were almost always available, and, in the summer months, the garden provided fresh vegetables. My mother always loved lemon cakes, pies, and puddings. She often made a dessert called "Lemon Fluff", using graham cracker crumbs, flavored gelatin, and whipping cream. Thinking back, we did not have access to fresh lemons so that is probably why it was such a treat for her.

Sylva's Lemon Fluff Dessert

1 can evaporated milk (chill 3 or 4 hours first)
¼ c. lemon juice (1 or 2 lemons)
1 pkg. lemon gelatin, dissolved in 1 ¾ c. boiling water
1 c. sugar
½ box vanilla wafers, crushed (2 cups)

Chill gelatin until partially set, and whip it up light and fluffy. Add lemon juice and sugar. Whip evaporated milk until thick and fold into gelatin. Grease pan (9 x 13 inches) and spread the bottom with crumbs; save a little. Add the gelatin mixture and sprinkle remaining crumbs on top. Place in refrigerator overnight. When ready to serve, cut in desired shapes. Put a dab of whipped cream and a maraschino cherry on each piece.

When I was a little older, we moved to 920 East 21st Street, near the entrance to what was then called McKennan Hospital, in Sioux Falls. The Lockwoods lived on the east side of our home, and Mrs. Keifer lived on the west. These three houses, plus the snack shop and Edmunds Grocery, are all part of what is now the Avera Hospital campus. Milk with cream on top was delivered to our house in glass mason jars by horse-drawn wagon, as was ice from Girton Adams Ice Company. Ice cut from the Sioux River was also available. There were iron trolley tracks in parts of the city, but the trains had stopped running by the time my memory got into gear. As a young child, I spent many hours on our front porch with my books and modeling clay. My dad purchased one piece of meat on Friday from Morrell's meatpacking plant to last through the next week.

Going to Grandma's in Hills, MN, 1932

We had a used 1938 Plymouth that took Dad to work during the week and the family to Hills, Minnesota, on Sundays – a cherished family drive to visit our Norwegian grandparents and have a delicious chicken dinner. As a special treat, the family would occasionally drive the Plymouth to Dell's Creamery, near the courthouse in Sioux Falls, and get inexpensive milk, five-cent root beers, and ten-cent floats. I do not remember ever getting a ride to Longfellow Grade School or Washington High School in the Plymouth. Grandmother on Mother's side died in 1940. This meant no more Sunday chicken dinners. Not only did I miss Grandma; I also missed those chicken dinners.

I remember reading two fictional series of books as a young boy. One was Franklin Dixon's *Ted Scott Flying Stories* - about an aviation hero who, in the first book, was the first pilot to fly over the Atlantic Ocean to Paris; another was C. S. Forester's *Horatio Hornblower* series - about the adventures of a Royal Navy officer during the Napoleonic War era. I must have read a hundred books as a boy. More than once teachers complained to my mother during school conferences that if I spent as much time on my assignments as I did reading books under my desk, my grades would be better.

Book-Lover (age 10) on the grounds of Hazelville, 1940

Jim and I, twenty months apart in age, shared a room on the second floor of our house. We also shared a ¾ size bed as kids, and all the way through high school. Betty, a sweet and pretty girl eight years younger than I, had her own room and her own interests that were different than my brother's and mine. The walls of Jim's and my room were covered with pictures of automobiles, trucks, and airplanes. We had many friends at school - mutual and otherwise. Recess at Longfellow Elementary School consisted of lots of games, with and without balls, and there was only one roll-on-the-ground fight that I got into. Dick Fry and I got along well thereafter.

My brother and I built model airplanes with rubber band-powered propellers, using wood, tissue paper, and glue. Mother was not always happy to share the tissue paper she used to make bouquets of colorful flowers with pipe cleaner stems. One day, she asked Jim and me to clear our room of clutter, including our flying airplanes. We figured out how to do this and have fun at the same time; we made sure the weather conditions were right and the landing area was clear, and then set each one on fire and flew it out our bedroom window. I think we were imagining that they were warplanes that had been shot down.

In 1946, my father became the superintendent of a new packing plant in Fremont, Nebraska. Dad went ahead without the family. He soon suffered what was then referred to as a "nervous breakdown" and became manic-depressive. His only treatment was receiving electric shock treatments, as this was a time before effective medications were available. Saving money became my answer to the concern about being the oldest child and having to support the family. Dad came back and, after some unemployment, became the manager for a time of a local Nash Finch Restaurant Supply subsidiary in Sioux Falls.

For me, numbers and dates have always been retained more easily than words. A detailed series of events that may occur in complicated business deals can be remembered - but as time goes by, names are blurred in my mind. Perhaps this is why I love history and chose it as my college major. I graduated from Washington High School (Dad's alma mater) in 1948 and started college at Augustana in Sioux Falls. Unlike many other students, my close friends (Jack, Roger, and Bill) and I did not live on campus. Due, in part, to his struggle with mental illness, my dad did not always have a job, and my family did not have a steady breadwinner. So I felt a duty to help support the family by working and saving while finishing my education.

Early during my education at Augustana College, I was taking pre-med courses and I intended to become a psychiatrist. I have quite a vivid memory of a session in psychology class with Dr. Jorgen Thompson. The topics covered in class that day were the personality traits of introversion and extraversion. During the next class session, Dr. Thompson asked all of us to guess whether our fellow students were introverts or extraverts. As it turned out, my classmates thought I was the most extraverted student in the room. However, when we took an assessment that measured these traits, my test showed that I was clearly an introvert. This surprised me too because, in addition to dominating many of the conversations I had with people, I had done a little acting throughout school and in the community. I had also spoken to a large group at the Sioux Falls Arena for a citywide career presentation. How could a young man who was clearly outgoing and who could talk a person's ear off be an introvert?

There was more of a tendency at that time to think of introversion and extraversion as being on opposite ends of a single continuum; if you were high on one of the traits, you were assumed to be low on the other. We thought of introverts as shy and reserved, and extraverts as talkative and energetic, like I was. Emerging at that time in the psychology of personality field of study was the idea that everyone has both traits, with one usually being more dominant than the other. Instead of focusing on how outgoing or quiet a person is when around other people, the more current perspective emphasizes what seems to make an individual feel more energized – being with others or being alone.

So, a person may not be shy (socially fearful) or uncomfortable in a social situation, and may be very talkative - but still might be more of an introvert, preferring to spend plenty of time alone for thinking and reflection. In her 2012 book, *Quiet: The power of introverts in a world that can't stop talking*, Susan Cain says, "introverts prefer to work independently, and solitude can be a catalyst to innovation" in the arts, business, and science. Entrepreneurs need to be creative and work at their own pace. This all makes more sense to me now; I realize I have always been quite introverted, spending a great deal of time thinking, planning, studying, and reading, in spite of my talkative nature.

My 20th birthday with friends Roger, Bill, and Jack - July 23, 1950

In college, reading became established as a lifelong habit. Books were my favorite because I knew that the author put a great deal of time and care into researching the topic. I loved to read then and, at eighty-five, I still spend many enjoyable hours reading books, newspapers, and finance-related magazines. Until a few years ago, I got by on 5 hours of sleep a night. Depending on the need to know, I would get up by 5:00 a.m. and read before going to the office. It was exciting to follow a learning pathway; for me, the morning was for these exciting discoveries. Since young adulthood, I have religiously read *Forbes Magazine* and *The Wall Street Journal*. I subscribe to *The Economist* for a world viewpoint. My family and close friends know that a book - especially biography, history, or economics - is always a welcome gift for me.

Augustana College, with its focus on liberal arts education, still holds a special place in my heart. In 1952, I graduated with a bachelor's degree in history. Following my 2-yr service as a lieutenant in the US Navy during the Korean

War, I returned to Augustana to earn a second degree, this time in economics. This allowed me to complete a master's degree in economics at South Dakota State University in 1966. On May 25th, 1997, I found myself dressed once again in cap and gown, this time humbled and honored to receive the honorary degree Doctor of Humane Letters from Augustana College.

Before I was given a chance to learn formal lessons at Longfellow School, Washington High School, Augustana College, or South Dakota State University, I learned about some important things while growing up in Sioux Falls, South Dakota: I learned about how families get along in tough times, and about what it feels like to be part of an extended family in a close and vibrant Midwestern community. We all bring into adulthood our childhood experiences, which give each of us our own unique perspective on the world and our place within it. The unstable financial situation of my family - as well as my introverted, yet outgoing, personality - had an impact on my decision to pursue a career as an entrepreneur. Another chapter of my life – the time I spent in the Navy during the Korean War - also provided experience that led me down that path.

CHAPTER 4

What the Navy Taught Me about Business

I'm glad I was in the Navy.

~ YOGI BERRA (B. 1925), MAJOR LEAGUE BASEBALL LEGEND

DURING MY EARLY SCHOOL YEARS, I played Phillip Nolan in *The Man Without a Country* at Longfellow School. This was also a period of Boy Scouting activities. I have many memories of Troop 43, including our weekly patrol meetings in the Longfellow gym, and my efforts aimed at earning individual merit badges. After earning the required twenty-one badges for the Eagle Scout rank, I had to earn five more merit badges to become a Star Scout. One of my responsibilities was being in charge of a Star Scout camp for others who also wanted to advance. There was a dinner dance for teenage Scouts, with girls invited. Maybe we learned a little bit about "girl scouting" from that experience. As a Boy Scout, if what I was doing gave me a feeling of accomplishment, it did not bother me if others thought differently about it. But it was always a concern to me personally when others did not take advantage of learning opportunities available to them.

Eagle Scout ceremony - February 10th, 1947
Chuck Thurston, me, Jack Seubert, and Pete Ried

During my Washington High School days in the mid to late 1940s, there were two jobs to do besides working for Uncle Doc and tending the family's tomatoes; both involved cleaning. One was to clean a downtown dress shop called KB. The other was "after-shift" cleanup of construction sites for Roger Schmidt's dad's home construction business. My friend, Jack Seubert, also had a cleaning job after school. The two of us watched the celebration of the end of World War II on August 14, 1945, from the roof of Kopel's, the Sioux Falls store he cleaned.

In high school, my friends and I often ate the lunches we brought from home at Lyon Park on the corner of Phillips Avenue and 14th Street, not far from Washington High School. You could find us sprawled on the grass near the restored Chesapeake Bay Cannon, which had been placed in Sioux Falls in the 1890s, and had been in service during the American Civil War. We also spent time drawing replicas of the Pacific Islands and outlining naval battles in chalk on our basement floors after school. We had several dozen three-inch metal navy ships that we used to approximate battle positions. Little did we know that several years later we would be doing it for real in the impending Korean War.

By the time I was a student at Augustana College, my Boy Scout experience had ended, but the US Navy Reserve took its place. My friends Jack Seubert, Roger Schmidt, Bill Ranny, and Walter Schrupt (US Air Force general) joined the military, and so did I. Most of us joined the US Navy Reserve, which met in an old air base laundry building. During my time in the Navy Reserve, I went to the Great Lakes Training Station, north of Chicago, and later to Jamaica on a US Navy destroyer, the U.S.S. Blue, where my duty station was sickbay. I remember being amazed to see the movie actor Errol Flynn sitting in a Jamaican bar with a group of people.

In a promotion photo (far left) on the U.S.S. Blue (DD-744)

I may not have thought about it at the time, but looking back I realize how the military helped form my business values. Clear organizational structure, effective training, quality well-maintained equipment, and dedicated crewmembers all contributed to the ability of a Naval ship to steam a steady course. The same is true for a business. A ship goes through charted but variable routes with full cooperation and planning from all hands. Success and failure are shared experiences. In the Navy, I learned both people- and equipment- organization skills that served me well in business. Each sailor has a role and each piece of equipment has a purpose and a place. The similarities don't end there but, obviously, the goals and tactics in war are different from those in a business. A ship and its crew are prepared for any defensive or offensive tactical opportunity. There are clear lines of authority from the captain on down. Anyone who is nervous at the helm is sent below deck immediately.

The U.S.S. Blue (DD-744) Naval Destroyer

Planning, communication, and calculation are constant activities in anticipation of battle conditions. A task force of 20 or so ships can work together, as well as individually, under additional layers of leadership, communication, and organization. Changes of personnel, procedures, and equipment are typically made only at the end of the journey or mission. Rarely are transfers made at sea. Compromising the main mission is carefully guarded against.

In 1953, during a military service dry dock period in Vallejo, California, I purchased a second rental operation 2,000 miles from home and called it Vallejo Rent All. Many military veterans apply skills and values they learned while in the military to run successful businesses. Veterans are taught that failure is not an option. In both the military and the business world, that often means putting in extra hours and making personal sacrifices. The work ethic enforced in the military can help veterans focus on the overall mission and help them complete tasks or solve problems, however daunting, with courage and tenacity. Previous military training can make a veteran more comfortable seeking knowledge from people with more experience, even if they are under that person's supervision.

Veterans are at least 45 percent more likely to take the plunge into entrepreneurship than people with no active-duty military experience, according to a May 2011 study from the Small Business Association (SBA) Office of Advocacy. The SBA study found that veterans with 20-plus years of service had higher rates of self-employment, and officers had the highest propensity to become self-employed. "This could be because military training develops organizational skills and risk-tolerance", says Thomas J. Leney, executive director for Small and Veteran Business Programs at the U.S. Department of Veterans Affairs.

"We rent most everything!"

Many years in the rental business have given me the chance to test some of the skills learned and the values instilled in me during my military training. In the Navy, I was responsible for all the anti-aircraft guns except the 5-inch. I also devised and implemented a procedure on Mare Island for checking out and tracking tools and equipment - a system that minimized equipment losses on my ship, the U.S.S. Blue. As a naval officer, it was important for me to delegate responsibilities effectively, and to share my ideas on how to accomplish the task at hand in the most efficient manner. As an entrepreneur, not being able or willing to delegate responsibility when needed can jeopardize the sustainability of your business model. Clearly communicating your business philosophy to everyone involved in the organization is of the utmost importance. The Navy taught me the importance of discipline and organization, and was good training for owning my own business - but persistence got me the girl of my dreams.

CHAPTER 5

Get Me to the Church on Time

—◆—

You've got to think about 'big things' while you're doing small things, so that all the small things go in the right direction.

~ ALVIN TOFFLER (B. 1928), AMERICAN AUTHOR AND FUTURIST

RELIGIOUS AND ETHNIC CUSTOMS HAVE always fascinated me. My Norwegian mother was a strict Lutheran from Hills, Minnesota. When her parents came to America, the Norwegian Lutheran church was a significant and conservative force in the upper Midwest. As is typical in other cultural or religious traditions, Sunday dinner together in the Norwegian community was an important part of family life. I remember these extended family gatherings from my childhood, and they continued until my parents no longer lived independently in their home. The meal served was often fried chicken or beef roast with mashed potatoes and gravy, along with side dishes brought by various family members. Dad would sometimes compete with his grandchildren for his favorite piece of chicken - the drumstick - and was especially fond of a piece of apple pie topped with a slice of cheese. My parents each shared some of their Scandinavian traditions when the family was together for the Sunday meal, for birthdays, and to celebrate holidays like Christmas, Easter, or Mother's Day. My mother never forgot the Norwegian table prayer that her parents brought with them from Norway:

I Jesu navn går vi til bords
å spise, drikke på ditt ord.
Deg, Gud til ære, oss til gavn,
Så får vi mat i Jesu navn.
Amen.
In Jesus' name to the table we go
To eat and drink according to His word.
To God the honor, us the gain,
So we have food in Jesus' name.
Amen.

My Swedish father was a Methodist, and my younger siblings and I were raised in the Methodist Church. I remember singing "The B-I-B-L-E" as a young child and being one of only three students left in Sunday school as a high school senior. Our folks were active in various church groups and activities at First United Methodist Church, which was, and still is, on South Spring Avenue in Sioux Falls. Dad was on the church trustee board, and they both were in charge of the annual fall festival fundraiser numerous times. Due, in large part, to his Methodist church affiliation, Dad was opposed to drinking alcohol of any kind; if wine glasses were part of the table setup in a restaurant, he would immediately ask for them to be removed. As uncompromising and vocal as he was about "the evils of alcohol" and a few other moral or political issues, he was a softhearted soul who typically only needed my mother (whom he called "mommy") to tug gently at his ear to calm down. When each of his grandchildren and great-grandchildren were small, Dad entertained them by crossing his legs and bouncing them up and down on his ankle, while holding their little hands and singing the following Swedish rhyme:

Rida rida Ranka
Hästen heter Blanka
Vart ska vi rida?
Till en liten piga
Vad kan hon heta?
Jungfru Margareta
Wheeeeee!

Ride, Ride the Pony
Pony's name is Blanka
Where shall we ride?
To see the little maid
What do we call her?
Maiden Margareta
Wheeeeee!

My wife, Rita, and I met in 1950 at a dance held at the Carpenter Ballroom in downtown Sioux Falls. She was beautiful, sweet, and a good dancer. After sixty-three years of marriage, she still has all of these qualities, and the figure of a twenty-year-old. Rita grew up in Madelia and St. James, Minnesota. She attended Swedish liberal arts college Gustavus Adolphus for two years before moving to Sioux Falls to work as a bookkeeper for McKean Buick. We danced together several times the night we met, and I was eager to drive her home at the end of the evening. Rita had come to the dance with several of her girlfriends, and declined my offer of a ride home so she could leave the dance with them. She did give me her phone number, but I couldn't bring myself to call her right away. When I finally called two weeks later, she was a little mad that I had not called sooner.

Augustana Graduation, spring, 1952 (l); Sioux Falls Airport after 6 months at sea, 1953 (r)

Rita and I wrote letters to each other during the first six months of my Korean War tour. I was both seasick *and* lovesick during our correspondence. Rita wrote less often than I did, and seemed less convinced that we should get married. I tried to give her some time and space, but I'm sure she could read through the lines and figure out that I was quite sure that I wanted to marry her.

.

Saturday, 3pm, July 28, 1952

Dear Rita,

Saw a wonderful show last night — "The Happy Time" with Charles Boyer. They will probably censor it in Sioux Falls, but it's very worth seeing.

Guess what - I just bought the complete outfit for my officer's wardrobe this morning. (The complete set, with an extra suit of khaki's and blues, plus 5 white shirts, costs $375.00.) I get all this on the 11th of August and will ship it home to the folks. Rita dear — would you tell the folks about it? It's really a nice outfit. Later on, I'm going to have a blue suit and a black suit tailor-made. There are only ready-made ones available now.

I'll really look flashy when we're together, but I won't have much time to enjoy it (10 days). We mustn't expect too much for those ten days just because we have been looking forward to it for so long. But I admit that it will be wonderful even if we don't do anything at all; someday, we'll be able to do everything together.

I love you so much that I dare not mention it to anyone, lest they think it impossible. I hope that you believe me.
Love, Bob

In my dress whites uniform

I started writing the following letter to Rita, and, after falling asleep, finished it early the next morning:

Saturday 9:45pm, July 28, 1952

My Darling Rita,

The lights are about to go out, but I have so many thoughts on my mind that I want to write some of them to you — the girl that I am in love with. I have been studying all night but so many things are always running through my mind. You will not understand what I want to say because I don't either, but I love you and I want you to know me from the inside.

Everything wonderful that I see, and everyone interesting and intelligent that I talk to, gives me inspiration that I believe no one will ever understand. People are very rash when they judge a person's motives — they judge them upon their own dull drives and material ambitions. One must be both educated and humble to become cognizant and sensitive to the real and full meaning of life. I have the intense desire (sometimes it is more powerful than any other desire) to become acquainted with that portion of the world that finds out things, knows about things, and does something about things. I realize my humble position in life (even though I don't act like it). I find good, and feel intense pleasure, in accomplishing things and becoming proficient in improving myself for something ahead, of which I do not even know. It is almost my religion and I have come to depend on it. Lights Out.

Sunday 6:30am, July 29, 1952

I slept an hour later this morning and it sure felt good. You're asleep now and it's a good feeling to know where you are. I'd like to be there.

Last night I felt so many things but it was taps and lights out before I could say any of them. I'll probably never think the very same things again but it was wonderful to see the way clear, even for just a few hours. Darling — I want to accomplish a lot of things in the next 30 years. It's going to be fun, thrilling, exciting and sometimes a little painful, but the important thing is that it will all be in one direction. All my efforts will point to what I believe in - a strong U.S, a good sound government, chances for people with talent, and chances for everyone to live and be happy. I'm the happiest man alive whenever I'm doing "good", getting ahead, making someone happy, etc. I have many faults, but, if I can just see the way ahead, I can become myself. For the next three years I'm going to work real hard to be a good officer. I'm going to save all the money I can so that I will not be cramped when I get out. I want a chance to make you happy. In short, darling — I'm going to get the most out of life and give all I can back to it.

I want you to understand that most of what makes me difficult to get along with is due to this underlying drive. Sometimes I wish that I could be normal and do nothing but please you and the people around me for the instant. I do what is feasible to do, considering the things that I have to stick to in order to be consistent with my plans.

Darling – I love you, and that is one of the things that I'm going to stick to.

XXX Bob

Rita doesn't look very sure about getting married.

Rita and I were married on November 15th, 1952, shortly after I returned to the Naval base in Long Beach, California. Our mothers rode out to California for the wedding in a 1952 Chevy with my best man, Jack Seubert, and Rita's maid of honor, Muriel Brewick. There were three naval "wedding packages" to choose from; the one I chose included a wedding cake and some electric candles wrapped in aluminum foil. That was as fancy as it got. I wore my officer's uniform and Rita wore a sharp grey suit that still fit her perfectly when she tried it on fifty years later. We were finally able to be together for six months at a time when I was in dry dock. We lived in a Quonset hut at Mare Island Naval Shipyard, 25 miles northeast of San Francisco. Mare Island was the first U.S. Navy base established on the Pacific Ocean.

This next letter was written after we were married. As an officer, I was now allowed the use of a typewriter, so Rita no longer had to decipher my messy handwriting.

SUNDAY, JUNE 28, 1953

MY DEAREST DARLING WIFE,
JUST GOT THROUGH SEEING THE SHOW "BECAUSE OF YOU" WITH LORETA YOUNG, AND JEFF CHANDLER. IT WAS SO GOOD BECAUSE IT SHOWED HOW IMPORTANT A WIFE IS TO HER HUSBAND, AND HOW IMPORTANT A MOTHER IS TO A CHILD. EVERYTHING IN THE WORLD WOULD MEAN NOTHING TO ME WITHOUT YOU RIGHT BESIDE ME DARLING. IT IS SO HARD FOR MOST PEOPLE (INCLUDING ME) TO GET INTO A FRAME OF MIND TO REALIZE A FACT SUCH AS THIS. THE MOST THRILLING KIND OF LIFE WOULD BE TO LIVE APPRECIATING EACH OTHER AND NOT JUST THINKING ABOUT IT FROM AFAR OR FORGETTING ABOUT IT WHEN WE ARE TOGETHER. IF I COULD ONLY WRITE DOWN ALL THE THINGS THAT I WAS THINKING ABOUT WHEN THE MOVIE WAS BEING SHOWN. IT'S WONDERFUL WHAT LIFE CAN BE LIKE IF YOU KNOW HOW TO EXPERIENCE AND TASTE IT. WE ARE SO LUCKY BECAUSE WE CAN HAVE SUCH A LIFE WITHOUT HUMDRUM AND FIGHTING FOR BARE EXISTENCE. ONE CAN LOSE BY HAVING EVERYTHING AND I HAVE A FIRM CONVICTION THAT THIS SHOULD NOT HAPPEN TO US.

SOMETIMES THESE FEELINGS COME TO ME WHEN I CANNOT GO TO MY STATEROOM AND WRITE THEM DOWN BUT I CAN GET AT LEAST A SMALL PERCENTAGE OF THEM TO YOU SWEETHEART.

I KNOW YOU HAVE TO WAIT FOR ME . . . I HAVE A JOB TO DO . . . MY DAYS ARE JUST AS LONELY HERE . . . AND MAYBE EVEN MORE . . . THAN THOSE YOU MUST ENDURE . . . DEAR ONE . . . ON OUR BELOVED SHORE . . . I WANT YOU MORE THAN EVER AND . . . IT MAKES MY POOR HEART ACHE . . . WHILE ALL MY THOUGHTS AND DEEDS ARE FOR . . . YOUR OWN BELOVED SAKE . . . BUT SOMEDAY, DARLING, THERE WILL BE . . . AN END TO ALL OF THIS . . . AND I SHALL TAKE YOU IN MY ARMS . . . AND GREET YOU WITH A KISS . . . AND IN THE SOFTNESS OF YOUR VOICE . . . AND SWEETNESS OF YOUR SMILE . . . OUR WORLD WILL BE THE SAME AGAIN . . . SO --- WILL YOU WAIT A WHILE?

MONDAY, JUNE 29, 1953

I LOVE YOU VERY MUCH HONEY AND I HOPE YOU ARE WORKING, WORKING, WORKING, WAITING, WAITING, WAITING, FOR ME LIKE I AM DOING FOR YOU. SOMEDAY WE WILL MAKE THIS ALL VERY WORTHWHILE.

XXXXXXX LOVE, BOB

Rita, and the 1952 Chevy, in front of our Quonset hut on Mare Island, 1953

When we moved back to Sioux Falls from Vallejo, California, in July 1954, Rita was seven months pregnant with our first daughter, Brenda, born that September. We joined Our Savior's Lutheran Church, which was on 33rd Street just south of Augustana College in Sioux Falls. This decision was not too difficult because Rita and her parents had attended churches that were part of the Swedish Lutheran Church in America synod in Minnesota, and I had a connection with the Norwegian Lutheran Church through my mother. All three daughters were baptized and married at Our Savior's Lutheran, which was a fast-growing church with many ways to be involved.

The family at Christmastime, 1967 - Brenda, Rita, Julie, Sarah and me

Rita served in ways that interested her, and I served on many committees. I also taught Sunday school for six years running (3rd grade - 8th grade) with a class that included our first daughter, Brenda. I liked staying with the same group, and learning along with them. The students and I got to know each other well over these years, and many of them have become outstanding citizens.

In recent years, my involvement on church committees has lessened, but I have become a sort of financial advisor on property matters for the church and its ministries. In my experience, churches and other nonprofit organizations are not always equipped to carry out complicated real estate deals. And regardless of the real and potential benefits of acquiring additional property, they often have trouble dealing with the concept of risk. To me, working out any complications of land acquisition in order to accommodate a growing and diverse congregation are very little work in relation to the benefit for the church. The fact that these things pretty much all connect for me in a satisfying way is my reward. Something of great benefit is better done - in spite of the challenges inherent in the process - than not done. Moving forward with worthwhile real estate transactions takes time, patience, and the ability to tolerate some uncertainty throughout the process, but churches fortunate enough to be growing need to anticipate their need for expansion and take the necessary steps to accommodate the growth.

In certain circumstances, it is not possible, or even necessary, for a church to acquire more property to meet the needs of the congregation. In the 1980's Augustana College and Our Savior's Lutheran Church, which occupy contiguous properties, were both dealing with parking shortages. I thought these two entities should share parking. After all, churches usually need more parking on weekends, whereas colleges typically have greater parking needs throughout the week. I helped arrange a cross-easement to provide the solution to parking problems for the two neighboring institutions.

In 2006, Rita and I attended a series of meetings on Martin Luther that were held at our church. Then, with the help of several of our friends, we hosted a weekly study group on the book, *The Purpose-Driven Life*, by mega church pastor Rick Warren. The small group of eight allowed for frank discussions about personal faith and the church. I was surprised to learn that Lutherans typically only invite someone to their church once every twenty-nine years! Someone suggested ("tongue in cheek") that maybe better results could be had if we were told to keep our faith to ourselves.

At every stage in my life, involvement at some level in my church has given me a sense of security and spiritual richness, and has provided a meaningful way to contribute time and business expertise to an organization whose mission I admire. In the January 2007 *Reader's Digest*, an eighty-eight-year-old man shared his principles for living in a story called "The Journey": "Be at peace with others, confess your faults, and overcome them with God's help. Treat others as you would want them to treat you. Guard your tongue; use it for good instead of evil. Never repay evil with evil. Avoid revenge. Do not be a captive of the past. Practice the power of forgiveness." These, along with the importance of sharing financial resources with the goal of making good things happen, are principles I strive to follow as well.

CHAPTER 6

The Great Outdoors

—⚏—

A ship in port is safe; but that is not what ships are built for.

Sail out to sea and do new things.

~ GRACE MURRAY HOPPER (1906-1992), NAVY REAR ADMIRAL AND COMPUTER

SCIENTIST

SUNDAY, DECEMBER 7, 1941, STARTED out like any other brisk fall day. My younger brother and I, along with Uncle Doc and several others, were hunting jack-rabbits in a two-square-mile area not far from Sioux Falls. The soft white fur of jackrabbits was an important cash crop for the ranchers in our area during World War II. Each pelt could be sold to the military for seventy-five cents. The fur was used to line military flight jackets worn by our soldiers, who need-ed extra warmth in the cold bomber planes. I remember being in the back of a large stock truck that day when we were told that the Japanese had attacked Pearl Harbor.

Bob, Jim (in white pants), & Uncle Ernest "Doc" Elmen - hunting on Pearl Harbor Day, 1941

I was eleven-years-old that cold day in 1941 when Pearl Harbor was attacked. Hunting was an exciting and important activity in my life at that time, has been since then, and still is today. Even so, my experiences as a both a hunter and as a sailor have taught me some important lessons about life. In the following paragraphs, I will share some of my thoughts - and a few stories - related to hunting and fishing. Along the way, I will highlight the ways in which each of these activities informed my business philosophy.

THE THRILL OF THE HUNT

The ring-necked pheasant was imported to America from Asia, and no other game species introduced to this continent has been as successful at flourishing as the pheasant. The Chinese knew the pheasant around 3,000 years ago, but the Romans are considered responsible for the spread of pheasants in Western Europe. When Julius Caesar invaded England in the first century B.C., the pheasant followed. The ringed-necked pheasant, easily identified by its colorful plumage, was brought to New York in 1733 and eventually to South Dakota in 1898. They were released near Brandon and Sioux Falls, and other areas in eastern South Dakota around the year 1919 (ultimatepheasanthunting.com).

The pheasant is now primarily a mid-western bird and is considered a delicacy in many other states. As many a pheasant hunter will attest, these birds are very crafty and will outsmart even the most experienced hunters on a regular basis. In some ways, the challenges inherent in pheasant hunting are not unlike those encountered in the business world. Timing, patience, creativity, and resolve are personal attributes that are necessary - but none of these guarantees success in either endeavor. Some of the early ring-necked pheasants in eastern South Dakota were raised in a brown chicken coop and pen on Uncle Doc's seven-acre property. Our local paper, *The Argus Leader,* ran a story in October of 1998 about the pheasants that were originally raised on land my family owned. Here is an excerpt from that article:

> The nationally known legacy of pheasant hunting in South Dakota had its beginnings over a hundred years ago with a Sioux Falls surgeon who loved the outdoors. Dr. Karsten A.L. Zetlitz made the first confirmed stocking of pheasants in the state in 1898, according to the state Game, Fish and Parks Department records.
>
> It was a modest but significant effort that included several golden and silver pheasants, which disappeared, along with two male and four female ring-necked pheasants, which were successfully established in the area. This marked the beginning of a stocking campaign in eastern South Dakota that would help the brassy imported Asian bird become a mainstay of fall hunting

and a flashy symbol of economic development. Long ago declared the state bird by the South Dakota Legislature, the gaudy ring neck now attracts up to 60,000 hunters from other states each year, as well as 70,000 resident shot gunners. The direct annual pheasant hunting income [in 1998] is estimated at up to $90 million.

Dr. Zetlitz couldn't foresee all that when he built a few pens outside his home on South Minnesota Avenue near what is now 19th Street. He eventually expanded his bird-rearing operation to land he purchased as a summer place on the shore of the Big Sioux River, just south of the Minnesota Avenue bridge. That location, now well inside the city limits, was far out in the country then. "He was a practicing surgeon who started Sioux Valley Hospital and was kind of a gentleman farmer," said Sheri Watke, an historical researcher in Sioux Falls. "He made the estate into kind of a nature area and named it Hazelville, for his daughter, Hazel, who had died."

Other stocking efforts were scattered across eastern South Dakota. And in the next few years the state got involved in the stocking campaign. By 1919 there were enough birds in Spink County for a one-day season, the first official pheasant hunt sanctioned by the state. By the mid-1920s, pheasants were common in much of eastern South Dakota, as was pheasant hunting. By then, Zetlitz had sold his property south of the Big Sioux River to a local dentist, Dr. Ernest Elmen.

When Zetlitz left town in 1925, he left a legacy that was carried on by the Elmens at Hazelville. Ernest (Doc) Elmen loved wildlife and used the pens for raising birds. Later, his nephew,

Bob, now a Sioux Falls businessman, spent adolescent days on the property, and still remembers the poultry shack and pens that since have disappeared. The Elmen family sold the property in several tracts in 1971, but the foundation of the poultry shack that adjoined the pens still stands in the thicket on the property. Bob Elmen stopped there one morning last week to remember his childhood days along the river and to marvel at the grand sport that began with a few imported birds and creative people, including Dr. Zetlitz. "It takes somebody different to try something like that. The regular routine doesn't include that sort of innovation," he said.

Horses were kept at the Hazelville estate so Dr. Zetlitz could rush to the hospital four miles north, or to make emergency house calls. Sometimes he would operate on a kitchen farmhouse table after a long horse ride. My family still has the heavy safe Dr. Zetlitz left when he moved to California in 1925.

During the period of World War II, my brother and I did a lot of pheasant and duck hunting with Dad, Doc, other relatives, and friends. We also sometimes hunted with the soldiers who were training as air force navigators at the Sioux Falls Air Base. A shortage of help on many farms in those days, due to the war effort's demand for labor, meant that cornfields did not get weeded as often and, consequently, that pheasants could more easily find cover in the fields. So there were many pheasants, some even in cornfields close to town, and plenty of opportunities to try to outsmart them. Jim and I also went on several two-day trips to the Missouri River to hunt geese with Uncle Doc, who had a passion for the elusive goose trophies. Hunting and fishing require a special state of mind - being attuned to yourself and the world around you. Our favorite fishing excursion when we were a little older was to drive north with Uncle Doc and sometimes Dad, and then fly into the Canadian lake chains to fish for walleye, northern, and trout.

Hunting, 1945 - Jim, me, Jack Seubert, and "Dottie" (in car trunk)

I have always been thankful that Rita understands about my being gone most years on our anniversary, which conflicts with the opening of deer season. November 15th is also the birthday of our daughter Julie, who was born on our 4th anniversary. I have heard my wife being lightheartedly referred to as "Saint Rita" a few times over the years; while I'm not completely sure what her "saint-hood" implies about me, my hunting and fishing excursions may be part of the reason.

A Navy buddy, Joe Huff, and I have been deer hunting together for many years. The two of us, my brother Jim, and other fellow huntsmen, have driven west across the state of South Dakota every November for deer season. Since 2001, the destination has been our three-square-mile ranch in the Buffalo Gap area along the Cheyenne River in Western South Dakota. There, you must see things - the weather, the landscape, and the prey - exactly the way they are, and then do your best to get good results. This often involves getting up at the crack of dawn, trekking a good distance from the cabin, and then hunkering down in the cold to wait for the deer. It is an exercise in self-discipline and patience.

My son-in-law, Bob Kopp, joined a few others and me on a November hunting trip to Buffalo Gap a couple years ago. After the group split up for what was meant to be a few hours one afternoon, I slipped while climbing through a barbed wire fence. Not only did I leave part of my jacket on the barbed wire; I also sprained my ankle badly and was unable to stand. Unfortunately, I had left my cell phone at the cabin that morning and could not get in touch with any of my hunting partners. We had planned to meet up again at two o'clock that afternoon, so, as darkness set in and the temperature dropped below 20 degrees, I knew they were looking for me. I shot my gun into the air occasionally, hoping that would help my cause.

As a light snow blanketed the ground where I had hunkered down against a tree, I could not stop shivering from the cold. I thought this just might be the end for me. While my exhausted mind was attempting to examine some high and low points of my life, and I was thinking of loved ones I might not see again - Rita, our children and grandchildren - Bob was contacting the local Search and Rescue team to help find his father-in-law. You would not be reading about this little episode if things had turned out differently. Fortunately, I was able to refuse the ambulance ride, and, while I felt bad about causing such a ruckus, one of my main regrets was that I had not gotten my deer before this all happened.

The Elusiveness of the Catch

I may not completely agree with author John Steinbeck when he quipped, "It has always been my private conviction that any man who puts his intelligence up against a fish and loses had it coming." But I will say that fly-fishing in particular is a very humbling outdoor activity - requiring patience, skill, and cunning. The fly-fisherman is trying to outsmart a slippery, unpredictable creature in its own environment - and he is at a distinct disadvantage, regardless of his IQ. I am afraid Rita and our kids are painfully aware of how many fishing ponds and trout streams there are just off the South Dakota highways - because I often felt compelled to stop the car and cast my line during family trips to the Black Hills. Rita has long been a prolific knitter, but my passion for fishing may be partly responsible for her habit of keeping her knitting basket in the car at all times.

Trout fishing at Spearfish Creek with daughter Sarah and "Hunting" Poodle, Tommy, 1975

One of my favorite fishing memories is a fly-in Canadian fishing trip with my son-in-law, Ken Gruys, and grandchildren, Hanna and Peter Elmen-Gruys. The trip coincided with our negotiations with the acquisition team for United Rental Inc. (URI) in the summer of 1999, and the timing was intentional; my brother and I preferred to let our attorney, Vance Goldammer, and accountant,

Tom Whalen, handle the details of the sale of our 47 stores to URI. For me, being far away on a fishing trip with my grandkids was just where I wanted to be - and it signified the transition to what I thought at the time would be at least a partial retirement.

In business dealings I try never to back anyone into a corner, but when I am fishing, it is a different story. I get so excited about bay fishing on my boat in South Padre Island, Texas, that I tend to hyper-focus on catching fish. Several years ago I found the perfect spot to drop anchor and throw out my line. Unfortunately, I failed to tie the anchor to the boat before throwing it overboard. ("Anchors away!") The bay fishing has been especially challenging in the past several years, with the fish population dwindling due to "red tide" - a naturally occurring, and higher-than-normal concentration of the microscopic algae *Karenia brevis*. This organism produces a toxin that affects the central nervous system of fish, paralyzing them so they cannot breathe. "As a result, red tide often results in dead fish washing up on Gulf beaches. When red tide algae reproduce in dense concentrations or "blooms," they are visible as discolored patches of ocean water, often reddish in color" (South Padre Island Department of Coastal Resources).

South Padre Island family fishing trip, 2015

In spite of the misadventure at Buffalo Gap and the many times my fishing line came up empty, the joy and satisfaction I have gotten over the years from hunting or fishing is hard to put into words. I can compare it with the satisfaction I get from closing a business deal. A well-prepared meal of walleye or trout at a restaurant cannot come close to the delectable experience of preparing a hard-earned catch of the day and sharing it with others who appreciate the experience. In the same way, I do not think winning the lottery would be as satisfying to me as striving hard, overcoming challenges, and seeing great results in business, even if the jackpot were much smaller.

CHAPTER 7

What Makes an Entrepreneur Tick?

—ɯ—

I knew that if I failed I wouldn't regret that - but I knew the one thing
I might regret is not trying."

~ JEFF BEZOS (B. 1964), AMAZON FOUNDER AND CEO

SEVERAL YEARS AGO I READ *The Hypomanic Edge: The Link Between (a little) Craziness and (a lot of) Success in America*, a 2006 book by John Gartner about energetic high achievers. Dr. Gartner views Hypomania as an inherited temperament, with some disadvantages that are outweighed by adaptive advantages. A hypomanic person may be boastful at times, and seem a bit "out there" with lots of big ideas – some clever and realistic, others less so. These characteristics may also be used to describe those of us who have started and run businesses. Successful entrepreneurs are creative people with infectious energy who typically think, talk, move, and make decisions quickly. We often work on little sleep and get irritated by what we see as "minor obstacles" – not understanding why others don't see "the big picture" or share our vision.

Retrospective studies of historical figures that exhibited hypomanic behavior have identified Alexander Hamilton and Christopher Columbus as prototypical Hypomanic personalities. Both made significant impacts (controversial in

Columbus' case) in their respective fields and were very colorful characters. If you are a small business owner, you may or may not find yourself somewhere along the spectrum of Hypomanic behavior, but you are likely to share a constellation of unique qualities with other entrepreneurs. As I discuss several of these qualities below, see if you recognize yourself. It would be unrealistic to expect any one person – no matter how successful – to possess a full measure of each of the following qualities. The fact that I am no exception to this rule will not stop me from sharing how some of the characteristics of my own personality have come into play throughout my long career in the equipment rental industry.

THE ENTREPRENEURIAL PERSONALITY

Characteristics often associated with the highly successful businessperson are leadership, maturity, patience, perspicacity (keen mental vision), robust health, individuality, unflappability, drive, initiative, abundant energy, an uncanny sense of timing, and often – but not always – a high level of educational attainment. Financial independence is a goal of virtually all entrepreneurs, even though achieving this goal does not free them from the burden of responsibility that comes with wealth. I cannot claim to be in the same entrepreneurial category as Warren Buffet or Jeff Bezos, but all of us who aspire to be highly successful in our respective business ventures tend to have the following personality traits.

A Goal in Mind: We establish goals and set out to achieve them with highly focused enthusiasm and dedication. There is not much that can lure us away from our plans for success, due to the irrepressible and compulsive inner drive that is often a common characteristic of the entrepreneur. Knowing how far to go to get the battle won (and reach a goal) without losing the war is a struggle the striver knows well.

There are two key things I like to remember when I have a goal in mind: First, I try to leverage my work by accomplishing at least three tasks at the same time. By economizing your effort, you might, for example, be able to write an article, think about how it could be adapted as a chapter in a future book, and outline the material to make it suitable for presentation in a class. A second, and related, idea is to identify at least three clear benefits that will result from your efforts toward the stated goal. These may be loftier than the three tasks you are accomplishing, and can keep you motivated if you get discouraged. In the example above, some of the benefits you might focus on are having fun, earning some extra money, and sharing what you know with others. If you can economize your efforts toward a goal – and keep the potential benefits in mind while carrying out the necessary tasks – you will have a much better chance of reaching your goal, whether it is a financial or a personal one.

Risk Tolerance: Managers of our equipment rental stores were graduates of liberal arts colleges, where we hoped they figured out how to be life-long learners. The managers who stayed with the company for many years were basically running their own businesses, but they did not mind being employed by someone else. They shared the risks and the profits of the business through our Employee Stock Ownership Plan (ESOP). Entrepreneurs and certain higher-level managers accept the discomfort of uncertainty, and tolerate – even embrace – the unpredictability that can come with the pursuit of ambitious financial goals. They carry, longer than others, the burden of not knowing the outcome of a business decision or strategy. In general, as we move up the scale of responsibility we bear increasing amounts of uncertainty for longer stretches of time. A business owner may have to wait years for his or her efforts to pay off. My observation is that risk and uncertainty in business create distinct pains and pleasures that prove to be undesirable to most people, but nearly irresistible to others. Suitability matters a great deal when it comes to choosing a profession. If you are contemplating life as an entrepreneur, it is worth spending some time thinking about how your abilities, motivations, and personal inclinations fit into the risk vs. certainty question.

Acceptance of Responsibility: Entrepreneurs thrive under the burden of responsibility, and are usually able to propel their way through a challenging set of tasks by tapping into the deep well of ambition driving their thoughts and actions. Some adults require a significant amount of supervision and reassurance in order to be productive. Their lighter burden of responsibility for the success of the company contrasts with the heavy weight others may wish to carry. Each of us is most comfortable at some point along this scale. It's important to mention here that if the entire workforce behaved like entrepreneurs, things would not go very smoothly at all. There is room for folks at either end of the continuum, and at the various points along the way. People with all kinds of motivational dispositions make important work contributions. The important point here is to examine your own motivations – as well as your willingness to bear the burden of responsibility for the successful completion of a work product or service.

Deferment of Gratification: Entrepreneurs know that deferment of gratification often accompanies their way of life. We typically spend a lesser share of our income on the consumption of goods and on recreation, and a greater share on building our businesses. The point could be made that working *is* our recreation. We understand that reinvesting in our businesses helps them grow. In fact, publicly traded companies that buy back significant amounts of their own shares on the open market often outperform the broad market – making these buybacks valuable indicators for investors (Investment Manager David Fried, *Bottom Line/Personal,* March 15, 2014*)*.

Something to Prove: It is not always clear to whom we need to prove it, and that probably does not matter. Entrepreneurs just seem to have this relentless need to achieve, to make things happen, to do great things. It drives us and motivates us. In my 20s, I made the goal of becoming a millionaire by the age of 40; I was so determined to reach this goal that I spent most of my waking hours figuring out how to do it. A high-achieving entrepreneur also often likes being thought of as an expert – one of the benefits of staying in the same industry for a while. When you spend years in the same industry, you learn its history. Knowing what has been done before can help you identify how the industry can and should move forward.

Unwavering Passion: The successful entrepreneur will always be reading and researching ways to make the business better. Our work inspires us and draws us like a powerful magnet. We feel at home doing it. Being an entrepreneur demands commitment and dedication – more than many jobs do. If you are ambivalent or only mildly enthusiastic about your product or service, you are not likely to be sustained through the highs and lows that will inevitably occur. If you find something you love enough to want to share it with others, the passion will fuel your efforts – even during times when things are not going well. Like most entrepreneurs, I have always been willing to put in extra hours to make the business succeed, because success brings satisfaction that goes far beyond making money.

Creativity: Entrepreneurs often come up with creative solutions that are the synthesis of seemingly unrelated ideas. My family sometimes asks me to stay on topic when I am talking, and I know it can be frustrating for them when I bring up seemingly unrelated thoughts or situations. But a certain idea often makes me think of several others that are related – at least in my mind. So, while I may be an exasperating conversation partner at times, I like to think that being a divergent thinker has given me an edge in finding creative business solutions.

Discipline and Perseverance: Entrepreneurs are proactive, not waiting for someone to give them permission. We are focused on making our businesses work, and we tend to look at failure as an opportunity for learning and improving. We may be happy with our product or service, but rarely fully satisfied. We have overarching strategies and are purposeful in outlining the tactics to accomplish them. Successful entrepreneurs are disciplined enough to take steps every day toward the achievement of objectives. I am grateful now for the work I was expected to do as a boy in order to contribute to the well being of my family. This instilled in me an appreciation for a productive day's work. While many American families still struggle to make ends meet, I worry sometimes about young people from more affluent families missing out on the chance to experience what it's like to make a meaningful contribution to the family finances.

Forward-Looking Approach: Successful entrepreneurs may stray from the road-map, but there is always one in mind. We have the ability to look at everything around us and focus it toward our goals. Ideas are constantly being generated about workflow and efficiency, people skills and potential new businesses. Having one project that's doing well is great, but the successful entrepreneurs I know do not rest on their laurels. Instead, they are constantly asking themselves, "What's next?" They understand that being a successful entrepreneur is a lifestyle choice, not a destination.

My grandchildren think this photo of me is humorous (and it is!) but I want them to know the importance of checking the direction of the wind before making decisions.

A January 2, 2015 *Wall Street Journal* article presented an analysis of recently released Federal Reserve data from 2013, indicating that the percentage of people under age 30 who own a private business is the lowest it's been since 1989. Analysts say this may be partly explained by greater financial challenges today than 24 years ago. The article claims that a 2014 Pew Research Center survey found that over 50% of 18-to-29-year-olds reported one or more financial problems in the previous year (Endangered Species: Young U.S. Entrepreneurs: New Data Underscore Financial Challenges and Low Tolerance for Risk Among Young Americans, by Ruth Simon and Caelainn Barr, *Wall Street Journal*, January 2, 2015).

The authors of the *Wall Street Journal* piece say that analysts also wonder if there is a lower tolerance for risk among young Americans now. This idea, they say, contradicts the widely held stereotype of Millennials as entrepreneurial risk-takers, and also troubles economists concerned about new business formation in 2015 and beyond. One such economist, John Davis (faculty chair, Families in Business Program, Harvard Business School), goes on record in the article, saying "We need start-ups not only for employment, but also for ideas."

It's clear that economic conditions are always evolving, and that the business world is very different now than when I started out as a business owner so many years ago. But I believe that young entrepreneurs must possess many of the same qualities that new business owners have always relied upon: risk-tolerance, discipline, determination, passion, perseverance, and creativity – to name a few.

CHAPTER 8

Seeking Strategic Risk

—⧖—

People who don't take risks generally make about two big mistakes a year.
People who do take risks generally make about two big mistakes a year.

~ Peter Drucker (1909-2005), management consultant,

educator, author

One of the advantages of living in a "college town" is that there are often enriching experiences offered to community members. As parents of three daughters, Rita and I attended a seminar years ago by Nicky Marone, author of *Women & Risk: How to Master Your Fears and Do What You Never Thought You Could Do* (1992). She spoke about the importance of encouraging daughters to become more comfortable with risk-taking. Fast-forward to the 2013 publication of Sheryl Sandberg's popular and provocative book, *Lean In*, and it is clear that for women (and men) who want to succeed in business, assessing and taking risks is still a timely topic.

Skiing at Terry Peak in the Black Hills with daughters Brenda, Sarah, and Julie, 1972

For a man born during the Great Depression, I seem to have more than my share of optimism. There are times when that optimism – combined with un-wavering determination - has gotten me into a bit of trouble. I have been known to run out of gas on a highway and have to walk to a farmhouse for assistance (but only twice). Another time, the engine sputtered and the car rolled to a stop in the middle of nowhere, but I happened to see a rusty gas can hidden be-hind a fence - with enough fuel in it to get the car restarted and make it to the next town. That was lucky.

Rita would occasionally ride along with me when I visited our stores in Rochester, Minnesota; we would stop overnight in St. James to see her parents, Harold and Sadie Hale. Rita had been on the road with me enough times to get a little nervous when the needle on the gas gauge got too close to "empty" – so when we were about 30 minutes from St. James and the fuel warning light went on she was concerned. If we went about 10 minutes out of our way we could get some gas, but I was sure we could make it to St. James on what we had left, and be on time for the planned dinner with my in-laws. I decided we would stop at a local gas station the next morning before heading on our way.

You could have heard a feather drop during those long minutes before we pulled up in front of Sadie and Hale's house. I was quite satisfied that I had been right to insist we keep driving when the warning light flickered on. I decided not to rub it in, as my wife had been a good sport, as usual. The next morning, we said our goodbyes and threw the overnight bag in the trunk. Eager to get on our way, I started the car and pulled away from the curb. We travelled exactly two yards before the engine died a slow death and I realized the car was completely out of gas. While there was no real harm done (except to my ego), I began to suspect that I was probably pushing my luck by taking risks merely for the excitement of a close call.

Financial risk is the chance that an investment's actual return will be different than expected. It includes the possibility of losing some or all of the original investment. The greater the amount of risk an investor is willing to take on, the greater the potential return. The reason for this is that investors need to be compensated for taking on additional risk. Regardless of how hard you work and how skilled you are at analyzing financial information, playing the stock market always involves a certain element of risk. As Nobel Laureate Daniel Kahneman has said, "The markets simply don't afford enough regularity to be totally (or even largely) learnable." We all have to make decisions in the light of incomplete information, so when picking a stock, we do our homework, try to assess the risk, and then we hope for some good fortune.

Against the Gods: The remarkable story of risk, by Peter Bernstein (1998), is a history of our efforts to understand risk and probability – from the early gamblers in ancient Greece, to the work of 17th-century French mathematician Pascal, and on to modern chaos theory. According to Bernstein, understanding risk informs everything from game theory to bridge building to winemaking. It certainly comes into play when making important decisions as an entrepreneur.

Understanding risk and having some insight into your own propensities related to taking or avoiding risks is useful to you as an entrepreneur who – by definition – has to be willing to risk loss in order to make money. In some ways, not taking a risk can be a risk in and of itself. As entrepreneurs, we often have to take strategic and well-timed risks in order to take advantage of an opportunity when it presents itself. Financial risk is more than just the likelihood of loss. It also involves assessing the *severity* of the potential loss, as well as the level of potential gain associated with any business decision. It's complicated.

We all know that time is money. I began to understand this as a boy, and became fascinated with the concept as I grew into young adulthood. The monetary value of an hour of work – less than one dollar, three dollars, five dollars, eight dollars, and so on – was an important point of reference for me as I worked in various jobs and made decisions about how to make the best use of my time. At some point I realized that if I continued to work for a set wage I may never earn enough money to do much more than merely support myself, let alone a future family.

One of my Augustana College professors, Dr. Fromke, once said that after college an A student would make ten thousand dollars per year, a B student five thousand dollars per year, and a C student five thousand to a hundred thousand dollars per year. This made me feel very good at the time, because I was struggling in a couple of my pre-med courses. I suppose one possible reason the C student may not be getting As is that he or she has a hard time staying focused on the material for the sole purpose of getting a good grade, preferring instead to engage in subjects that seem more relevant and exciting. That same student may be attracted to the idea of becoming an entrepreneur, a career that requires taking calculated risks in the hope of reaping great rewards.

I did not always get "A"s, except for a span of time back at Augustana after the Korean War, when I took more business courses in order to be able to attend a graduate program in economics. One of my undergraduate chemistry class-mates, Charles Wright, has said that I told him in class that I wanted to be a mil-lionaire someday. This fits with my memory of studying in Old Main Library as a sophomore and deciding to change from pre-med to business courses. I wanted to learn how to obtain and grow assets for my family, and for my old age. It was becoming more and more important to me to be able to work for myself, not someone else – and to work at my own pace.

I remember thinking that the goal of eventually making enough money to consider myself secure and successful did not mesh well with the idea of "serving mankind", which now seemed more like a luxury I could not afford. I decided that, if I were going to make it, from then on I would have to focus on working hard and working efficiently. This almost became a game for me. I usually read five hours a day, but not always for my lessons. When I had done the required preparation for classes, and clocked the expected hours at one or another of my jobs, I tried to have time to read about subjects related in some way to the coursework I would be tested on. The object of the game was to learn as much as possible about everything that interested me, and still get "B"s or better.

There was never enough time to read or do everything that my curiosity or imagination set me out to do. Therefore, at an early age, I began to pick out things that I wanted to explore further. Somewhere along the line, it became apparent that some things had to be left out because I worked hard to finish whatever was started. Sometimes learning has less to do with a prescribed program, and more to do with figuring out how to get the best work out of yourself while moving steadily toward your goals. As American entrepreneur Jim Rohn said, "Formal education will make you a living; self-education will make you a fortune."

Keeping track of national trailer rentals in the early 1950s

It has never bothered me to think my own way through to a solution. Once I was in college, it became increasingly clear that to build any level of financial security I would need to learn how to make my hard-earned money work for *me*. There was just no way to do this without becoming comfortable with taking some calculated risks – investing in more stocks and bonds that I hoped would help me accumulate wealth. The fear of losing money was always present, along with the possibility of making a profit on any investment. (After all, the counterpoint to risk is opportunity.) But, there was another way to potentially gain some financial leverage – starting a business and investing time, effort, and money in the venture. This was also risky, but at least I would have some control over how this investment turned out. I could work hard, learn from day-to-day successes and failures, and make decisions that would optimize the chance for making a profit.

CHAPTER 9

You Name It – We Rent It!

—⚏—

To be successful, you have to have your heart in your business -
And your business in your heart.

~ THOMAS WATSON (1874-1956), CEO OF
INTERNATIONAL BUSINESS MACHINES (IBM)

THE MODERN EQUIPMENT RENTAL INDUSTRY emerged as a response to post-World
War II American optimism. People were moving across the country to take
advantage of new opportunities. Young families needed trailers to move their
belongings, as well as tools and equipment for fixing up new homes. The
do-it-yourself trend had taken hold, but small contractors were also renting
equipment to build homes, offices, bridges, and roads all across America.
It was during this era that I decided to learn to become comfortable with
risk and become an entrepreneur. This decision put my life on a whole new
trajectory. Over the next fifty-plus years I learned a great deal – from both
successes and failures.

Our first South Dakota rental store location at 2012 West 12th Street in Sioux Falls

In early 1950, my father saw an advertisement in the local newspaper and sent for a brochure about opening a United Rent-Alls equipment rental franchise (no relation to United Rental, Inc.). On September 15th of that year, with our pooled savings, Dad, my brother Jim, and I opened a small rental store at 2012 W. 12th Street in Sioux Falls. The building rent was thirty-five dollars per month - but the owner, Mr. Kutil, wanted three months' rent in case it did not work out. We were glad the property had a small lot in back where we could keep larger rental items. Moberly Print Shop and Eberly Refrigeration Service were two other businesses nearby. Five years after we opened the store, we purchased three lots at 1701-15 W. 12th Street and built a new forty-by-eighty-foot rental building. Before long, we put on a two-story addition and transitioned to private ownership of the business – not realizing at the time that we would sell 47 rental stores to the publicly traded United Rentals Inc. (URI) some 50 years later.

After college graduation - and while I was based in Mare Island, California with the US Navy - we purchased property and a rental store at 205 Benicia Boulevard in Vallejo, California. I was spending 6 months at a time on a US Naval Destroyer in Korea, so I hired a retired naval officer to manage the store for a time until third-class petty officer and friend Joe Huff - whose Naval commission had, by then, expired - could assume management duties. Joe eventually moved from California to Sioux Falls, where he settled and raised a family.

He was a dedicated employee of our company until his retirement many years later, and has always been a good friend and hunting partner.

By 1956, we were farther along on the learning curve and ready to be serious about investing more in the rental business. We opened a branch store on East 8th Street in Sioux Falls that year. The inventory for this store was furnished from the home store on West 12th Street. I remember being paid half the net income of the new store for my wages. The branch store in Sioux Falls and the Vallejo, California store were giving us experience in managing multiple loca-tions and in handling operations from a distance. *Replicating our business model in other geographic locations - and adapting the model for use in other related business ventures - would become an extremely important component of our company's success.*

We opened the first Minnesota store, Rochester Rent All, in 1959. All cash flow was left in the business. Cash from the sale of Vallejo Rent All to Ted DeVries in 1962 also went back into the business. The Sioux Falls business was reorganized in 1960 as a Subchapter S Partnership called Elmen Rent All Inc., owned by Dad, Jim, and myself. Several diverse companies, one being trailers throughout the United States, were combined into two Rent All lo-cations in Sioux Falls. That year (1960) we partnered with C. Verner "Gus" Gustafson to open the St. Paul, Minnesota operation, which eventually grew to include stores in Anoka (1973) and North Suburban (1974) in the St. Paul area.

It seemed like we were always short of money, and we never wasted a dime if we could help it. Even so, we added equipment and usually added new locations of rental stores each year. We borrowed money in the spring, and paid it all back by year-end. The banks would loan us up to twice as much the following year. This was our secret weapon, if there was such a thing. Borrowing money was always a risk, but the uptick in equipment rentals that typically occurred in the non-winter months gave us the boost in business that helped us pay off the bank loans. We did our borrowing at local banks in Sioux Falls "because for many years going 300 miles in any direction would have cost us 1% more" (*Little*

Business on the Prairie: Entrepreneurship, Prosperity, and Challenge in South Dakota, Robert E. Wright, The Center for Western Studies, 2015)

When Dad resisted purchasing riskier equipment, brother Jim and I secretly bought a large Rototiller, and kept separate track of its rental income to avoid alarming him if it didn't earn its keep. In 1966, we purchased a store in western South Dakota (Rapid City), and eventually made as much per dollar invested in that as in our base store. During the next several years, stores were purchased in four Iowa cities - Sioux City (1970), Mason City (1971), Des Moines (1972), Cedar Rapids (1973) – and in Grand Forks, North Dakota (1973). By this time 12 stores, geographically dispersed throughout the Midwest in a four-state region, were operating and new managers were being trained to allow for continued expansion.

"You Name It—We Rent It"
The Reader's Digest, July 1966.

"Following World War II, when millions of do-it-yourselfers were busily improving their homes, some unknown handyman had to fix his roof. He found that it would cost him $30 to buy a suitable ladder, but that he could rent one at the hardware store for $1 a day. Since he seldom used a ladder and since his storage space was small, he decided to rent.

The decision was catching. His economy-minded neighbors were quick to follow suit. They, too, began to rent instead of buy items for which they had only occasional use, such as lawn rollers, sanding machines, floor polishers, and punch bowls.

Their activities were being duplicated throughout the country. To supply the demand, hundreds of pioneers, many of them war veterans who wanted to turn their own businesses, soon were plunging into the equipment-rental field. Unlike the specialized shops, which had been renting certain kinds of equipment for more than a century, many of these newcomers offered to rent almost anything. "You Name It—We Rent It," they proclaimed. The rental revolution had begun.

Rental businesses tend to be family-run. Many were started on a shoestring. Another successful family venture is Elmen Rent All, Inc. in Sioux Falls, SD, a city of 65,000 surrounded by rich farming country. 'When I got out of the Navy in 1950,' says Robert C. Elmen, 'Dad answered an ad and got a pamphlet about how to go into the rental business. My brother joined us, and we started with $10,000 worth of equipment (plus a few items Dad owned for his personal use) in a building we rented for $35 a month. Now we have five stores and rent out everything from mink coats to pitchforks.'

The Elmens have 500 trailers (for cargo and camping), which are on the road most of the time. They do a big business renting boats. Also popular are 20 wire hoopskirts, which women rent to wear under bouffant dresses at weddings.

But the franchise system, popular in other service fields, plays only a small role in this one. Nine out of ten dealers operate independently. As Robert Elmen says, 'No one would work as hard as we do for anyone else.'

In September of "66, Elmen published Some Operational Aspects of the General Rental Industry, which he sold for $10 a copy. Used as the basis for his masters' degree, Elmen's book was based on five years of research and 16 years in the equipment rental business. The book was viewed as the most authoritative book on the rental industry up to that point. It sold out of the initial print run within the first month, leading to a second printing.

There are many cities in the United States with populations larger than the entire population of the state of South Dakota. Once our equipment rental business concept was profitably organized in South Dakota, we set about to replicate the model in more densely populated areas in the Midwest. We avoided opening stores in cities where we were not likely to dominate the market within a reasonable time period. Our locations were typically main street frontages instead of side street destinations. We tried to purchase properties where interstate and main highways intersected, and we timed store openings to combine advertising campaigns in multiple-store areas. We would save one portion of each property for a potential later sale, use a second portion for a rental store, and a third portion for a self-storage facility. The self-storage business was managed locally by the rental store manager, with the added benefit of plenty of space in which to keep seasonal rental inventory.

I had noticed as a teenager that people who owned property did very well over time. This also proved to be true for us. My brother and I never passed up the chance to buy additional property on our main street rental locations. If we had to, we stretched for the required down payments, and we borrowed. We had excellent credit because we borrowed money each year to cover rental equipment needs from April to September, and always paid it back at year-end. This way, we only had to pay interest for half the year, and we could usually borrow up to twice the amount each succeeding year. Property was the ideal inflation hedge.

After our expansion plan was carried out we focused instead on consolidation; our goal then became to double business volume while scaling back the addition of more stores. From 1950 to 1975, a 25% compound growth rate was maintained, and the number of employees had grown from one to one hundred. Between 1955 and 1975 our volume had increased one hundred times over. By 1973, the business had grown beyond what could be handled on an individual store basis, and the need emerged for a system that could efficiently manage the diverse interests. At the end of that year the office began to handle actions across all locations in a more uniform way, and we developed procedures that all of the decentralized operations would follow. We tried to keep central office costs down to 3% of the growing firm's rental gross. Over the next few years, the stock grew at a healthy rate, and we began to see the benefits of running a more efficient operation.

We constructed an office building across the street from our main store on West 12th Street in Sioux Falls. The new Elmen Enterprises building was initially staffed with two bookkeepers, one secretary, and an accountant. Later, a marketing manager, computer programmer, and inventory specialist were added. Even when we grew to 49 stores, our central office was as small as any in the rental business. Some rental chain operations half our size likely had double our staff. Elmen Enterprises had become, in effect, decentralized operationally but centralized financially. With accounting, payroll, and other back-office services based in Sioux Falls, store managers were freed up to concentrate on the many operational aspects of their businesses, and on improving customer service. In addition, it has always been my belief that the centralized back office system helped eliminate the need for middle management.

In the earlier years, much of the central office work started with cash register tapes from each store and ended with a handwritten tax return. As computer and software technology was developed we had point of sale data to work with from each operation. My younger brother and business partner Jim took a hands-on approach to the business. Among many other responsibilities, he handled acquisition of rental equipment inventory and supervised store staff. A quick thinker and clever problem-solver, he was also in top physical condition - perhaps because he rarely stood still. Employees gave him the nickname "Jimmy Jet" because on some days he would jet in, repair a complicated piece of equipment in no time flat, talk to customers, address any staff-related issues that needed taking care of, go over the numbers, and then jet out again. I focused on management consultation, talent recruitment/hiring, store openings, and property acquisition/management. Risk assessment (insurance) and legal services were not based in-house, but were coordinated from the central office for all store locations.

During the 1980s, the equipment industry flourished in the wake of new tax laws implemented early in the decade. Rental businesses were able to take advantage of new investment tax credits and higher depreciation allowances. Likewise, renters benefited by writing off rent payments and, in many cases, reducing their effective tax burden. As a result, renting of all types of equipment surged. Office equipment rentals, for instance, grew more than twice as fast as overall business investment in new equipment during the 1980s (http://www.referenceforbusiness.com/industries/Service/Equipment-Rental-Leasing-Elsewhere-Classified.html).

"Rentals for the Excitement",
Rental Equipment Register
July 1983, by Ron Broch

South Dakota may not be a horn of plenty, but for the Elmen family it's been the base of operation for one of the world's most successful independent rental chains. Rental entrepreneur Bob Elmen doesn't like money per se. He likes excitement. 'Excitement comes when you make money', he told RER recently.

At Elmen Enterprises, rental stores provide excitement and a high return on investment; real estate is acquired as a hedge against inflation; mini-storage facilities act as a tax shelter; and computers help eliminate middle management for a chain of 25 stores. That's to date and the future is ripe. 'We're ready to grow. We've got the energy, finances and ideas. We're always poised to do something.'

If such a thing as a success formula exists, Elmen says the key ingredients are structure and logic. 'I'm a structure bug. A rental store must incorporate a logical management system if success is to be achieved. At minimum, a logical system will do half of your work and will monitor the other half. Store managers who can't build a logical system can only progress their businesses as far as they can see, touch or yell.'

Work modes have changed over the years for the Elmens. Until 1960, Bob, Jim, and Lloyd all worked behind the counter, in the shop, or wherever they were needed. It was difficult, according to Bob. But that year, he and Jim purchased two-thirds of the company from their father and roles changed. 'We each did something different, and the division of labor worked out better. It was logical,' Elmen said. 'Dad waited on trade and did a lot of worrying; Jim handled acquisition and maintenance of equipment, and supervised store staff; I monitored finances, worked on strategic planning, and looked for investment opportunities.'

Bob stresses close analysis of all financial data as a prerequisite for sustained profitability in the rental business. Perhaps most important, he said, is the rental manager's knowledge of his equipment winners and losers on a per-item basis. We grade our equipment on an 'A' through 'F' basis using our accumulated data. Basically, we compare original item cost to the year-to-date income it produces. That transforms to per-item information about turns,' Elmen explained. 'We can also check this against maintenance costs.'

Elmen acknowledged that their stores must keep many marginal items even though they're not good income producers. 'We'd like to start a museum for some of them,' he said. But they dump the real losers.

'Our goal is to have 'A' items in every store and maintain our volume with 'B' items. Eighty percent of our income comes from the 'A,' 'B' and 'C' items. We carefully watch our 'D' equipment, and we try to sell or transfer the 'F' items. We've always known if a particular store was making or losing money. Now we have the capability to work on a per-item basis to improve profitability at every outlet.'

After four years of compiling this detailed data, the Elmens are developing an equipment history profile. This helps prevent misjudging certain items, especially those affected by varied economics and weather conditions.

'We probably save $500,000 yearly with this information,' Elmen said. 'The data also tells us where to change our prices. There is a right price for everything and you have to know what it is.'

The Elmens further use this data to select equipment brands when purchases are made. 'The difference between one product and another is often the difference between a profit and a loss in the rental business; margins aren't that large', according to Elmen. 'Our in-house data make equipment purchase decisions for us, eliminating much of the guesswork.'

When it comes to the expansion of Elmen Rent All throughout North and South Dakota, Minnesota, Iowa, Nebraska, and six other states, there's a method to the madness. Again it's data. In this case, it's outside data.

Area tax laws are reviewed along with census data. Cities with a population under 30,000 aren't considered. Aerial color photographs from Earth Resources Observation Systems (EROS) in Sioux Falls are also used for site selection. 'McDonald's pays $10,000 for a single site study. We spend $15 for a photograph,' Elmen said. 'We don't mind the unconventional approach.'

'We pick our locations from the vantage point of whether we want
two or three stores in town—depending on where the competition is—and determine a fit. By looking at the aerial photograph, we have a vantage point that we can't get by talking to a
salesperson or by driving down the street. We keep in mind that
we're the ones who are trying to start a business — not the person who is selling us the property.'

The Elmen philosophy is to build enough outlets in an area to
cover the entire market, to open stores that don't clone each
other. Their strategy is market coverage and promotion.

In 1975, our 25th year in business, we wrote a retrospective company charter to
help managers, stockholders, creditors, and family better understand the organization. The document outlined the basic operating formula of Elmen Enterprises.
It was time-tested, and we rarely departed from the fundamentals outlined in it.
We revised the charter in 1985 to reflect policy changes in response to becoming
a more mature company. The document also provided a historical record up to
1985 that has been helpful to me as I write about those years.

Between 1970 and 1984 (when all the separate business activities of Elmen
Enterprises were combined) the total volume increased from $1,000,000 to
$8,000,000. Profits to gross were two times the average for the industry and
the equity to total assets were twice the rental industry's average. This left the
rental stores a little unleveraged but with a strong balance sheet. By 1984, 28
rental outlets were in operation in 12 markets.

My brother and I owned 50% or more of each firm (comprised of a main store
and its local branches), with the balance of ownership coming from store managers and equity investors. Keeping the firms separate was a lot of work, but, at
the same time, made it easier to motivate individual managers to improve their
stores and develop their businesses. The segmentation of firms also made de-
termining profits and losses more clear-cut, and figuring out manager bonuses

a more straightforward process. In addition, it enabled tax savings that more than equaled the total cost of running the central office.

We regularly put time and effort into strategic planning and assessing progress toward goals set at group manager meetings. I particularly enjoyed designing new business operations as we looked for ways to take advantage of any worthwhile future business or investment opportunities. We also kept abreast of economic conditions – especially anything relevant to the rental industry - and occasionally did research that we hoped would benefit the rental industry in general, as well as our own firms. For example, we studied inflation and its unique effect on the rental business. Simply put, inflation is an increase in the overall level of prices for goods and services - which typically leads to a decrease in the purchasing power of cash for those goods and services. While the effects of inflation may seem rather straightforward when thinking about the value of many consumable or durable goods, it is less straightforward when assessing the value of rental equipment.

It was very difficult to figure out how inflation really impacted our bottom line. I was not satisfied with how standard accounting practices addressed the issue of equipment depreciation costs from year to year while inflation was also occurring. Our replacement cost for five- to seven-year-old equipment was 50 percent higher than the allowed depreciation deduction. When we could, we spent money on repairs instead of on replacement. This issue must have also affected the farming and contracting industries, which also had to calculate the real cost of equipment in order to analyze company performance and track profits on a yearly basis. Due, in large part, to what we learned about the inability of standard accounting practices to accurately measure depreciation in our business, my brother and I shifted our emphasis somewhat from investing in rental stores to investing in real estate.

Rental stores were always the main event, and required a lot of capital to start and maintain. However, investments in property as well were important to the successful operation of the rental business. Each manager, as a local expert, was responsible for property management in his city. Almost all of our purchases included land that had potential independent of the intended use at the time. In the short run, bare land was the worst investment, but in the long run, it served as an inflation hedge and helped guarantee the survival of the main business.

Elmen Enterprises has used investment tax shelters for the protection of property and rental operation income. In 1973, the company opened its first self-storage facility as such a shelter. The Mini Stor-All venture was bittersweet - bitter because the tax shelter plan didn't exactly work out, and sweet because the business broke even and eventually made money. As an added benefit, the storage units provided plenty of space to house rental equipment in the off-season. Self-storage facilities were often integrated with rental store branches and were typically located on contiguous property.

The companies outside of Sioux Falls were called 'name of city' Rent All Inc. The name "Elmen Rent All Enterprises" included all 12 rental markets. It was a fictitious name and there was no tax return or official status; it merely represented a sum of the separate parts for credit support and management studies. The RIBOB & ELJIM Companies are Living Trust partnerships that have provided investment arm support for the rental operations, and were used for diversification, reserve, and collateral. The funds were invested in stocks, bonds, rental yard land, and buildings. As one of the first rental companies to embrace computerization, we developed the R.E.N.T.S software program, and provided user support to rental businesses that implemented the program.

Along with our successful ventures, we also had some fortune-sized losses to deal with. After a $5-million loss in our rent-to-own business, we put in numerous Dollar Etc. Stores, and they lost another $5 million. We lost a fortune buying futures contracts in the late 1990s. An assisted living center turned out to be a poor investment. A new kind of cement block building system did not work out for us either. We purchased a TV station and invested in many towers throughout the state. After many years of significant losses it is finally making money. Several property purchases turned out to be bad investments due to subterranean issues. At one time we were setting up a mail order service to ship high-turnover rental items to small towns and resort areas throughout the U.S. that couldn't support a storefront rental center. Plans were to set up distribution points in three geographic areas. After investing considerable amounts of time and money to get this off the ground, we realized our efforts would not pay off and decided to abandon the project.

In spite of numerous failures, our company grew and prospered. For this we credit the free enterprise system, and the important contributions of our talented managers and dedicated employees. Our mission has always been about working together toward the shared goals of service and profit. This simple philosophy provided guidance for all company decision-making for over fifty years.

CHAPTER 10

Gather your Team and Listen Well

—ꙮ—

Human beings, who are almost unique in having the
ability to learn from the experience of others, are also
remarkable for their apparent disinclination to do so.

~ Douglas Adams (1952-2001), English writer/humorist/dramatist;
author of The Hitchhiker's Guide to the Galaxy *(1979)*

Theodor Reik - one of Sigmund Freud's students in Vienna, Austria - fled
Nazism in 1938, came to America and practiced his own brand of psychoanaly-
sis. (Freud once asked Reik," Why do you piss around so much? Just piss in
one spot.") In *The Third Ear* (1948) Reik says "nothing said to us, nothing we
can learn from others, reaches us so deep as that which we find in ourselves."
While it is true that the answers we find within ourselves, and the lessons we
learn on our own, are invaluable - there are also many important things to be
learned from others. I have certainly found this to be the case throughout my
60+ years in the equipment rental industry.

Whether you are just starting your business, growing your business, or getting
ready to sell your business — you are likely to benefit from having a team of
people at your disposal with specialized skills and knowledge. Employees – full

or part time, permanent or temporary – will be hired because they can offer expertise that will help your business succeed. But not everyone on the team needs to be on the company payroll. Some professional roles (accounting) tend to be filled by part- or full-time staff but could also be contracted for with an agency that provides "back office" services; others (attorneys, independent consultants) may only be hired periodically on a fee-for-services basis. Still others (insurance agents, bankers) will provide professional advice at no cost, as long as you have a formal client relationship based on an account with their company.

Sometimes you just need to run an idea past someone whose judgment you trust. Board members and professional or trade association colleagues often have a unique perspective and useful advice to offer. And let's not forget the important advisory or support role family members and friends often play in our entrepreneurial endeavors. Being open to learning what you can from the specialized team you have assembled, as well as from people in your life who want you to be successful, will almost certainly increase the chances that your business will survive and thrive.

We may all use the same general language and live in the same world, but each field of endeavor has it's own lingo and specific practices. It is your job to learn the "language" of each of the disciplines that are important to running your company. You need the professional services and expertise of accountants, lawyers, insurance brokers, bankers, etc., and they need your business. You would do yourself a great favor by summoning the curiosity and imagination of your youth when you interact with the people your business depends on for continued success. As they say - listen and learn.

Dinner with Attorney Vance Goldammer, Banker Leonard Dankey,
Accountant Tom Whalen, with spouses.

ACCOUNTANTS

When you are in the process of establishing a business, there is a long list of ways an accountant can help. He or she can: 1) Assist with the financial analysis in your business plan; 2) Determine the best business structure (i.e., sole proprietorship, LLC, corporation, partnership) for your situation; 3) Advise you on the type of accounting software you may need; 4) Make sure your accounting procedures comply with government regulations and requirements: 5) Provide advice on how to track expenses for daily business activities; 6) Oversee company payroll and payment processes; 7) Help ensure that any independent contractors are not classified as employees by the IRS; 8) Provide advice on making estimated tax payments throughout the year; 9) Determine when, and to whom, to send W2 and 1099 forms; 10) Close out your books and create financial reports at the end of the year; and 11) Compile and submit taxes, financial reports and all necessary paperwork to the IRS.

If your business does well and enters a growth stage, your accountant can be an invaluable source of advice and help as you manage the growth process.

He or she can help you: 1) Determine specific areas for growth by providing insight on cash flow patterns, inventory management, and pricing; 2) Make decisions regarding property and equipment leasing and purchase; 3) Minimize the chance your business will be audited by the IRS; 4) Prepare for an IRS audit, if necessary; 5) Create financial forecasts so you can make better decisions in your business; 6) Create a budget that will support your expanded business goals; and 7) Sell your business. Remain cognizant of the sometimes-conflicting roles professionals may have to play. For example, you expect your accountant to be looking out for your financial interests, but he or she also needs to make sure that your business practices are legal and ethical.

While bringing in "new blood" can sometimes step up your accounting game, there is also value in having a long-term employment history with a capable and trusted accountant. Our firm's principal accountant, Tom Whalen, has been with Elmen Enterprises for nearly 40 years, and has been an indispensible member of our team. To benefit from the best of both worlds - and to make sure your business is using the most up-to-date accounting practices and rules - be sure to provide professional development opportunities for in-house professional staff.

LAWYERS

Another valuable team member with whom we've enjoyed a long-term professional relationship is our attorney, Vance Goldammer. I was his first client when he started out as a new attorney at an established firm. He hadn't even been assigned an office the first time I met with him; our meeting took place in a conference room that was also used by the administrative staff for making copies. Vance's legal expertise has been an essential component in virtually all of our company's business dealings and property transactions over the past 4 decades. Despite the many jokes about lawyers, Vance and other legal professionals I have worked with have proven themselves to be ethical, intelligent, and trustworthy.

If you are just getting your business off the ground, you will be focusing on the myriad tasks required, such as marketing, hiring, and so on. While all of these things are certainly high priority, be sure to include legal issues on your priority list. You might wait until you have a broken water pipe before calling a plumber, but don't wait until you have a legal problem before finding a good attorney. A smart business plan includes making sure the company is protected against potential legal trouble. Better to prevent a legal headache than to find yourself in the middle of one without skilled legal counsel. By the same token, be sure to consult your attorney right away if you think you may be heading onto shaky ground. A minor headache can quickly become a monster migraine.

Good lawyers are expensive, as is any other consultant critical to the success of your business, but at the very least, set up an appointment with an attorney for a brief consultation, with the goal of identifying the legal needs of your business. Think of it as a fire inspection or a medical check-up. If you are just getting started, a lawyer will help guide your business through the process of incorporation, and can help make sure it maintains corporation status. Failure to carry out the requirements of your particular state, such as holding annual shareholder and director meetings, recording of meeting minutes, and election of officers could jeopardize corporate status.

In addition to helping get your business entity established and avoiding legal issues, having appropriate legal safeguards in place can also give your business a competitive edge in the marketplace. One important consideration is protecting the intellectual property of your business; a good lawyer can advise you on how to protect your company's name, its logo, and other intangible assets that may be eligible for trademark, copyright, and patent registrations. And, depending on the nature of your business, you may need to set up non-disclosure and/or non-compete agreements with your employees. An attorney can assist you by drafting suitable employment agreements that guard against trade secrets being shared with the competition in the event an employee leaves your firm. If your closely held company (one with a small group of controlling shareholders) consists of a partnership, it might be wise to have an attorney draw up buy-sell or buy-back agreements, so that partners can sell their shares without legal complications, and so that an undue financial burden does not fall on the business should one or more partners or shareholders leave unexpectedly.

INSURANCE AGENTS

I like to talk to two or three agents when I'm in the market for any insurance policy. Nine times out of ten, this has helped me get competitive rates and has also educated me about the insurance product I am in the market for. Salespeople (not just those selling insurance) will want to connect with you. You will need to connect with some of them, and might want to continue the dialogue if the information helps you in any way. As a general rule, I don't rely exclusively on what a salesperson tells me about any product or service; I typically try to consult other sources to corroborate what I've been told.

There are many factors that determine the insurance needs of a business, including your business activities, location, business structure, and whether or not you have employees. Navigating the plethora of business insurance laws and best practices can be confusing, especially when much of the information on the internet comes directly from insurance companies or agents, who have a vested interest in convincing you to buy a policy. There are two basic types of business insurance: employer insurance, which is required by law, and commercial business insurance, which may or may not be required. You must provide Workers Compensation Insurance for your employees, and pay Unemployment Insurance Tax on their behalf. Businesses in one of six U.S. locations - California, Hawaii, New Jersey, New York, Puerto Rico, or Rhode Island - are required to have Disability Insurance for their employees.

While structuring your business as a Limited Liability Corporation (LLC) might protect your personal assets from business liabilities, you also need Business Liability Insurance to protect your business from events like theft, lawsuits, natural disasters, or the death of a partner. Familiarize yourself with the insurance laws in your state to see if your particular business activity requires you to purchase a specific type of insurance policy.

BANKERS

In securing funds for your business at its various stages, you are likely to work with more than one lending institution. Take advantage of the opportunity to learn what you can about the lending process, and continually increase your knowledge of financial fundamentals. The lending process works better for all involved when you plan for your financial needs well in advance.

Simply stated, the banker is in business to make a profit derived from the difference in the cost of funds made available to his or her institution and the rate of interest charged for qualified loans. The bank is in a "win only so much" position because potential gains, should you default on a loan, are limited. Your lender holds a more secure part of the investment, is not involved in the day-to-day aspects of your project, and doesn't get to enjoy the excitement (or the anxiety) that comes along with entrepreneurship. That said, think of him or her as a financial partner in your business venture. The relationship is symbiotic; the bank is providing funds that you need to stay in business, and you are keeping the bank in business. While in recent years credit has become tighter, bankers still want to grant a loan to a qualified borrower.

When you need a business loan, be sure you are able to clearly state what your financial needs are, as well as how the loan will contribute to the success of your business. It is important to keep your banker fully informed about all events, both good and bad, concerning your financial health. Dependable, accurate, and timely financial statements on your business and personal assets will be needed when a bank audit takes place, and will go a long way toward building your banker's trust in you. We appreciated the efforts of our now-retired banker, Truman Phelan. A steady record of trustworthiness is very important for continued and increasing credit availability.

You will, of course, consult additional sources for the most accurate and up-to-date information about how any of the professional specialties discussed here can help you and your particular business. But it's clear that having excellent accountants, lawyers, insurance professionals, and bankers on your team can move your business forward in the best way possible. Soak up as much specialty-related knowledge as you can from all of these people. The more we learn from others, the more likely we are to find important answers within ourselves.

CHAPTER 11

The Harder I Work, the Luckier I Get*

—ɯ—

Luck affects everything. Let your hook always be cast; in the
stream where you least expect it, there will be a fish.

~ Ovid (43 BC-14 AD), Ancient Roman poet and mythologist

If Ovid were here today, I wouldn't argue with him. Opportunities can easily
go unnoticed if we are not scanning the horizon for them during all of our working (and most of our *waking*) hours. While luck - or the even more fortuitous
"serendipity" - is often part of the equation, it would be foolish to rely too much
on either. Whether fly-fishing or seeking a financial fortune of any size, luck will
play a role, but the outcome will always depend on showing up and making an
honest effort. In a 2013 study from Spectrem Group, the wealth research firm,
some of the wealthy said luck played a role in their success, but more said hard
work, education and risk-taking played a role. Maybe we all like to think that our
successes are earned and that only our failures are due to luck — bad luck, that is.

Usufruct is a legal term (originating in 17th century Roman law) granting the
right to temporarily use and enjoy the profits of another's property, as long as it
is not destroyed or disposed of. At age ten I took advantage of usufruct rights,

---

* Samuel Goldwyn

often picking mulberries from a public garden on the grounds of McKennan Hospital, where small garden plots were also made available to local families. I planted radishes, beans, tomatoes, and other vegetables. When the plants could be harvested, the family ate the least attractive, but still nutritious, produce. The rest was placed in my small wagon, which I pulled around our part of town, selling bunches of radishes for five cents and beans for ten cents a pound. The very best tomatoes were sold to Edmunds' Grocery at ten cents a pound; I'm pretty sure I was the only produce supplier that stopped by the grocery every day to replace any bruised or spoiled tomatoes. Any remaining tomatoes were either sold to the hospital kitchen near our house, or canned by my mother for winter consumption.

Mother had many recipes that called for tomatoes. One of my favorites was her tomato soup. We didn't know it at the time, but Mother's simple recipe had the added benefit of being a rich source of lycopene, an antioxidant nutrient found in cooked tomatoes. Apparently, the number and size of tomatoes to start with is left up to the individual cook.

Mother's Garden Tomato Soup

Tomatoes, peeled or unpeeled
¼ tsp. baking soda
1 cup (or so) milk
Butter
Salt and Pepper

To peel tomatoes, drop them into boiling water for 15 to 30 seconds so skin slides off easily. Simmer peeled tomatoes in a pan until soft. When done, stir in ¼ teaspoon baking soda and continue to simmer. (Add no water to tomatoes.) Scald (not boil) milk in another pan; then add tomatoes to the milk. Put a piece of butter in soup bowl before ladling soup into it. Season to taste.

The income from our family garden on the grounds of McKennan Hospital helped keep my family fed and clothed. One year, there were one thousand irrigated tomato plants. The next year, three thousand plants were set. A very important lesson was learned when the increase in the number of plants meant that irrigation had to be supplemented with hand watering. The net profit was more important than the gross income. Since childhood, I have planted tomatoes every year except during my service in the Korean War (1952–1954). In very recent years, I've tended to tomato plants in a garden plot at our self-storage facility on 41st Street in Sioux Falls. One of the self-storage customers saw me harvesting the tomatoes one day and commented to the Mini Stor-All manager that it was "very nice of Mr. Elmen to let that old man pick his tomatoes" - not realizing that the old man *was* Mr. Elmen.

Harvesting garden tomatoes before I became an "old man"

Dad's oldest brother, Ernest "Doc" Elmen, was a prominent Sioux Falls dentist with a busy practice at 127 S. Phillips Avenue. Jim and I – both energetic boys - were in great demand at his seven-acre estate two miles south of 26th Street. There was always work to do on the grounds, which extended from South Minnesota Avenue to the banks of the Sioux River. Doc would sometimes ice skate the eight miles to and from his sixth-floor dental office downtown. In those days, the elevator always had an attendant.

My brother and I learned that work was often combined with adventure; along with taking care of grass, trees, and gardens, there were rabbits and squirrels to hunt on the estate, and fish to catch in the Big Sioux. I now realize that the opportunity to work without being able to compare our efforts with those of others gave us a chance to develop our own high standards. Jim and I would run from one end of the grounds to the other in order to complete various tasks, because we did not know that we were being paid for "travel time". We found out years later that it took two workers to replace what one of us did in taking care of whatever Doc asked us to do. No wonder Doc and Blanche "threatened" to adopt us. Working for Uncle Ernest ("Doc") was satisfying, but Uncle George was a city commissioner, and I was offered a job working for the City Parks Department. The work seemed too easy, and I found it frustrating to work at such a slow pace. So, for a nickel more an hour, I went to work on the night shift for the canning department at Morrell's meatpacking plant. (I'm sorry to say that I have not been able to eat a hotdog since then.)

I also did lawn work for Harold Bills, and construction site cleanup for Roswald Nearman. The foremen at these companies took me aside and told me that I had to slow down. Later in life they became my friends, and they kidded me about working so hard. In my heart, it was clear that it would not do to be in a situation where I worked at a job with parameters in its description. Once, I had a temporary job as a shoe salesman at Johnson Shoes in downtown Sioux Falls. The owner told me that I sold more shoes that day than any of his regular employees. I explained that I observed people in the crowd during the sale, and tried to determine which ones looked ready to buy. Then I focused on those customers. It has always been fun for me to figure out a better way to get something done, no matter what the situation might be.

The work of taking care of the lawn, trees, and flowerbeds of Doc and Blanche Elmen eventually became a full-time summer job. One thing I was learning from earning a set hourly wage was that taking care of trees and flowers, selling shoes, or processing meat at a packing plant was not "all roses", even though the work was manageable. I realized that I didn't want the amount of my paycheck to be limited by the number of hours I had worked.

In *Juicing the Orange* (Harvard Business School Press, July 2006), authors Pat Fallon and Fred Senn contend that the only way to generate measurable results is through good old-fashioned hard work. Using the term *Creative Leverage* as a metaphor for connecting with your creative genius, they advocate doing rigorous research, not taking anything for granted, and combining the thoroughness of the left-brain with the artistry of the right brain. I like their formula for success: Hard Work + Creativity + Strategic Risk + Luck = Success.

We've all heard some version of the saying, "Luck is what happens when preparation meets opportunity". One night quite a few years ago my brother and I were on the way to our Cicero Peak Ranch in the Black Hills when two spark plugs failed on the Suzuki Jeep we were driving. Thinking we were doomed (as this was before the invention of cell phones), we coasted up behind another Suzuki Jeep on the side of the otherwise deserted gravel road. The driver of that Jeep needed a tire jack in order to change a flat tire, which we had – and he happened to have extra spark plugs for us. It wasn't long before both vehicles were able to pull back onto the road and continue on. What were the odds of that happening? We and the other fellow were prepared for emergencies - just not the right emergencies. That's where the luck came in handy.

Hard work, persistence, creativity, and luck - all of these qualities play a role in seeking financial success. The 17th annual World Wealth Report revealed that people in North America with at least a million dollars in investable assets had climbed to 3.73 million. Is a millionaire considered wealthy? "A UBS survey found that nearly 70% of investors with income over $1 million in investable assets don't think of themselves as wealthy. Instead, most respondents believed

it would take at least $5 million in personal wealth to be considered wealthy."
(*The Wall Street Journal*, July 27, 2013)

Making more money than is needed for one's own consumption is not for everyone – and is certainly not possible for many people.   My own decision to pursue the goal of income beyond what my family and I required for a comfortable life is undoubtedly rooted in my desire to avoid the financial insecurity I experienced throughout my childhood and adolescence. Since then, I have read everything I could get my hands on concerning business, real estate acquisition, and entrepreneurship.   Consequently, our company library has accumulated many books on economic principles, business practices, investment strategies, and other related topics.

If you have entrepreneurial aspirations, you will know, or should know, that identifying and refining your ideal financial need-effort-goal combination is an ongoing process. Regardless of the type of business venture, you are going to succeed on the basis of what actually happens - not on what might happen, or even on what appears to be happening. This is why it's important to have a good understanding of business fundamentals and to learn how to adapt the fundamentals to a wide variety of situations. No two ventures will ever be alike, and one needs to be on firm ground conceptually when analyzing the possibilities. There are many fine books and courses that can be explored if knowledge about basic business principles is needed or desired.

Be aware that economic conditions and business parameters are always changing. If you are in the habit of wearing blinders as you forge ahead with your planned business activities, be sure to assess your progress on a regular basis, and seriously consider examining potentially problematic elements of your plan. You may need to change course, for example, by economizing or obtaining more capital. And long-term plans may have to be adjusted due to tax law changes. Remember that earned income is heavily taxed, so if you have a high salary or large business earnings you will have to shelter this income in a manner that satisfies your standards, as well as those of the IRS.

Many years ago I attended a Berkshire Hathaway annual meeting as a proud stockholder (of one share). I drove to Omaha, Nebraska with a friend from Sioux Falls who had twice as many shares as I did. (He had two.) Admirable or not, it has always been my goal to become wealthy. Over time, investing wisely in real estate, business ideas, or the stock market can create tremendous wealth, but all of these endeavors require time, dedication, hard work - and just plain luck.

CHAPTER 12

Investing – A Letter to My Grandchildren

—ɯ—

Be who you are and say what you feel - because those who mind don't matter,
And those who matter don't mind.

~ Bernard M. Baruch (1870-1965),

American financier and investor

Many people are familiar with Bernard Baruch's "Be who you are and say what you feel . . ." quote - sage advice that could just as easily have been written by Dr. Seuss. I may be the only person who memorized another of Mr. Baruch's comments, which appeared in *The New York Times* when I was a teenager in 1946. He said, "A small bit of information that makes sense and is not yet included in the broker data is more important than the information that is already baked into the price of the stock." As a sixteen-year-old worrying about how I would pay for college, my interest was piqued when I realized investing in the stock market might be something I could do to make the wages I was earning from part-time jobs increase in value over time. The idea that being successful in the stock market would require digging for and analyzing information that could give me a competitive advantage over other investors appealed to me as well. The plan would be to learn while I earned.

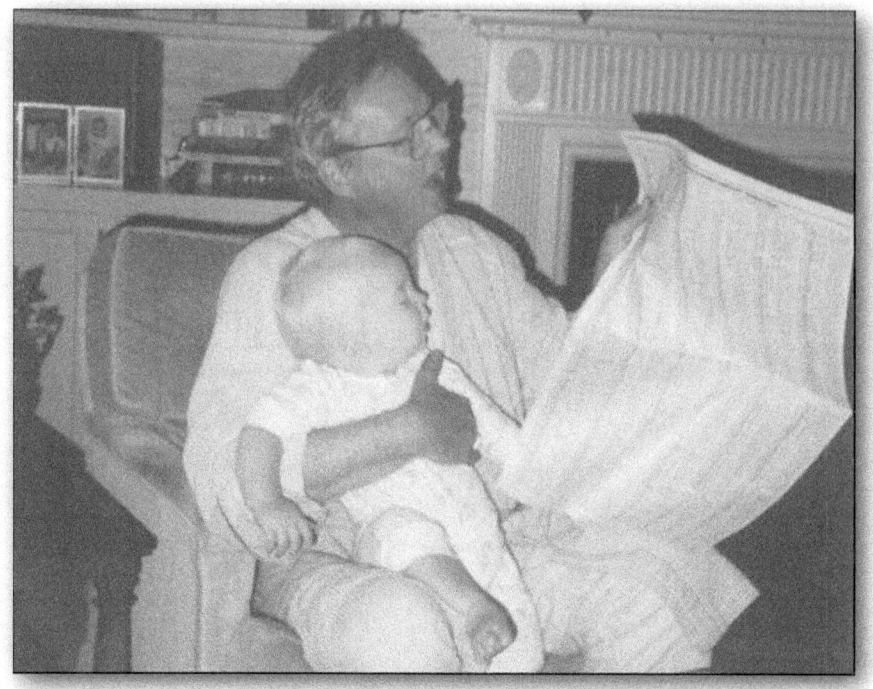

Checking stock prices with grandson Peter, 1992

My uncle, Ernest "Doc" Elmen, was able to offer me some useful coaching on stock investments. He purchased his stocks by telephone from a Merrill Lynch broker in Minneapolis. At the time, a close family friend named Ray Hunter owned the barbershop downtown where I got haircuts. The shop was located next to a stock exchange location that would later be replaced with a Piper Jaffrey office. An employee or broker at the counter would take your order for stocks at the exchange. Dow and Standard & Poor's books were available to look through, as were brochures for some of the stocks. While I waited in line for my haircut I would watch a big blackboard on which stock trades and up or down market changes were scribbled in chalk. This is where I placed my first stock order: 1200 shares of AT&T, 300 shares of Chrysler Corp, and 150 shares of Canadian Imperial Oil. I followed my three stocks very closely, and - armed with Bernard Baruch's advice not to rely on broker data alone - read everything I could find about each of these companies.

Fast forward to 1994, when I was appointed by the Legislative Research Council to a five-year appointment on the South Dakota Investment Council, which manages the financial assets of the state - including the South Dakota Retirement System, the School and Public Lands Fund, and the Healthcare Trust Fund, among others. During the last two years of my appointment, I served as chairman of the council. Nearly fifty years earlier, Uncle Doc had given me the dose of confidence I needed to try my hand in the stock market. He and Aunt Blanche didn't have children of their own, and I was fortunate to be the recipient of advice and encouragement from my uncle that, in different circumstances, may have been reserved for his own son.

In the following letter to my grandchildren, I hope to pass along some of what I learned about investing from Uncle Doc many years ago, and from my own experience in the decades since then. At the very least, my aim in writing this letter is to encourage my grandchildren to take an active role in managing their finances. And - in whatever they do - I hope they remember that " . . . those who mind don't matter, and those who matter don't mind".

Dear Grandchildren,

Your grandmother and I have taken great pleasure in being included in your lives. We are proud of each one of you, and have enjoyed learning even more about you in recent years. More than a few times you have paid your grandfather the honor of requesting advice concerning financial investments. I was 16 when my small savings were invested in three stocks, and it always pleases me to hear that the younger generation is planning for the future.

You will each figure out your own path to achieving financial security — taking into consideration your tolerance for risk, your ability to learn from mistakes, and many other variables. Not all of these variables will be within your control, but having a grasp of some core investment principles will be helpful nonetheless. I would like to share with you some very basic investment terms and strategies that have served me well during nearly seventy years of investing. I realize, of course, that you will want to seek current professional advice when the situation calls for it, but additional study on your part will be worthwhile.

Saving. First - and this is very important - set aside enough money in cash (that you've saved consistently from your hard-earned income) and income investments (like stocks with a high dividend that provide a steady infusion of liquid funds) to handle emergencies and near-term goals. Setting aside an emergency (or reserve) fund is one of the first and most important steps you should take to safeguard your financial stability. The idea is that you won't have easy access to the fund for everyday purposes. It will just sit, earning interest, until you're facing either a major unexpected cost (such as medical expenses) or the need to cover your basic living expenses if you (or your spouse or partner) loses a job or gets laid off. Interest rates are currently very low so it may seem counter-intuitive to keep cash in an interest-bearing account, but the main purpose of this fund is to provide security, not to produce interest income.

Exactly how much money you should keep in your reserve fund is open to debate. At an absolute minimum, it should cover your daily living expenses for three months. Six months would be wiser, and some planners recommend a full year. Just how cautious you want to be depends on your personal circumstances and what it takes to give you peace of mind. If you'd reach for your credit cards in an emergency, and would then end up paying 15% interest on the debt, you'd be better off saving enough to cover expenses for at least six months. And if your income fluctuates – if you're self-employed, for example - you'd do well to have a bigger cash cushion.

If you have the opportunity to decide between putting money into your reserve fund, paying off credit card debt, or funding your 401(k), start with the credit card debt. There's no point in having your own money sit in a bank earning 1% interest while you're simultaneously paying 15% interest to use someone else's money. Contribute to the 401(k) next. This is especially true if your employer offers a match; not taking advantage of it would be turning down free money.

Compound Interest is a basic and powerful financial concept that can greatly magnify the results of your investments. Albert Einstein once said, "Compound interest is the eighth wonder of the world. He who understands it earns it... he who doesn't... pays it." Compounding in finance refers to the ability of an asset to generate earnings, which are then reinvested in order to generate their own earnings. Compound interest is different from simple interest because simple interest applies only to the original principal and not to any other interest that has been previously earned. That is why, given the same interest rates, compound interest will grow a principal amount much faster than simple interest.

Don't feel like you have to create your entire fund this week. Most people start by setting aside a monthly amount -- for example, 5% of their paychecks, or another amount that lets them build up one month's worth of living expenses over the course of a year. It helps to make this automatic, for example, by asking your bank to set up an automatic deduction program from your checking account to your savings account. Also monitor your monthly spending, and look for areas you can trim. And if you receive any promotions, work bonuses, or other unexpected windfalls, pay down any credit card debt, and then think first about adding them to your emergency fund -- before you get used to spending the extra money.

Allocation. Putting all your eggs in one basket is a risky strategy. It's important to spread your money around by allocating portions of it to different investment categories. This protects you from losing all your assets in a falling market. Ideally, you should have some of each of the following: stocks, bonds, real estate funds, international securities, and cash. Investments in each of these different asset categories do different things for you. Stocks help your portfolio grow. Bonds bring in income. Real estate provides both a hedge against inflation and low "correlation" to stocks -- in other words, it may rise when stocks fall. International investments can provide growth and help maintain buying power in an increasingly globalized world. Cash gives you and your portfolio some stability.

Sixty percent of investment performance comes from a decision on asset allocation. So, for example, you may have 65% of your portfolio invested in stocks, and the rest in bonds and cash money market funds. A younger person with a longer time horizon might allocate up to 80 percent of his or her investment portfolio in stocks, because bonds and cash are generally more subject to the effects of income taxes and inflation. We typically diversify by investing one-third in closely held businesses, one-half in 'stocks and bonds', and one-sixth in real estate, leaving the rest in cash reserves. Each category by itself is a risk, but the combined asset portfolio has produced a dependable financial return over time.

Diversification. In addition to being aware of asset allocation, you also need to know how to diversify within a particular investment category. This protects your portfolio from being devastated when a single industry - say, financial services or energy – goes through a lengthy rough period. How do you go about diversifying? One relatively cost-effective way to start a diversified portfolio if you have less than about $150,000 to work with is to buy mutual funds. This strategy will minimize the trading fees you'd pay if you were buying individual stocks.

Mutual funds are managed investment pools that combine the money of many investors to buy stocks, bonds, real estate, and international securities. Index funds purchase all the shares of a particular index, such as the stock market's Standard & Poor (S&P) 500 Index of big company stocks. There are also bond index funds, international index funds, real estate index funds, and money market funds.

An Exchange-Traded Fund (ETF) is an asset that's flexible like a stock but offers the diversity of an index fund. ETFs usually track a particular commodity, industry, or market. They are not actively managed like mutual funds so they typically have lower administration costs; consequently, they often trade commission-free. Since they are less likely to experience the trading of securities, ETFs generate lower capital gains taxes and can yield a more efficient overall return on investment. In today's market, one fairly simple way to earn approximately 9% compounding interest is to invest in an ETF that tracks US stock indices.

Sector Weighting is based on what companies actually do, and accounts for roughly thirty percent of successful investment performance. There are three broad categories under which the various sectors fall – Information, Services, and Manufacturing. While there are other sector classification systems, these are the 2014 weightings for each of the ten sectors in the S&P 500. Technology: 18.43%; Financials: 16.07%; Health Care: 13.18%; Consumer Discretionary: 11.77%; Industrials: 10.7%; Energy: 10.7%; Consumer Staples: 9.99%; Materials: 3.5%; Utilities: 3.22%; and Telecom: 2.45%. Most, if not all, of these sectors should be represented by the stocks in your portfolio.

Individual Stocks. Only about ten percent of investment performance comes from the selection of individual stocks. I've always liked to purchase individual stocks in even 100-share lots, and I try to come close to the recommended percentage sector weightings listed above. You are all busy people and don't necessarily share my near-obsession with the stock market. Your grandmother will attest to the fact that I like to have the TV tuned to a financial channel like CNBC while the market is open, even while on vacation. I regularly check the financial news that might affect the stocks I own or am interested in. I spend up to twenty five percent of my waking hours studying and closely watching about 135 stocks and bonds, but keep far fewer than this in my investment portfolio.

Six well-chosen stocks can give you 85% diversification. You could expect to spend about 15 minutes a day keeping track of six stocks. Interestingly, if you have more than 19 stocks, not only will you probably spend a lot of time managing them, they will tend to transgress to the mean in performance. Depending on your situation, if the designated allocation of stocks, bonds, and cash in your investment portfolio is appropriate for your individual situation, and your holdings are diversified among the various sectors, I might recommend that you just buy and hold for the long term. That said, remember that Stocks aren't magic. Even if you hold them for a very long time, risk doesn't disappear.

You might also use no load liquid municipal mutual funds and money markets to buy stocks when they go down 20-30%. No one knows for sure when this will happen, but you can be prepared for the inevitable if you maintain some liquidity. In general, it's better to "buy" advice from someone who does not sell anything than to buy a financial product from someone offering "free" advice.

Keeping track of and managing an asset portfolio is a big responsibility. I hope you will exercise financial common sense so you can experience the freedom and independence that comes with financial security. I am confident that you will each continue to learn what is necessary in order to manage your financial resources, whether great or small. Take good care of your future, and always remember that Grandma and I love you very much.

Grandpa Bob

CHAPTER 13

An Employee Stock Ownership Plan

———∽∿∾———

A goal without a plan is just a wish.

~ ANTOINE DE SAINT-EXUPERY (1900-1944), FRENCH WRITER, POET,
AND PIONEERING AVIATOR

OUR MANAGEMENT SYSTEM HAS BEEN central to the way we have conducted business. Service-oriented and labor-intensive businesses cannot operate in a multi-state area without a system of management that, in effect, takes the place of the owner's eye. We hired college graduates with a major in any field of study. They needed to be able to tackle, with confidence, the broad and varied tasks of the job. They typically had at least a bare minimum of mechanical aptitude, an ability to get along with people, and a basic understanding of accounting practices. They also had to be trustworthy - a good test for this being the ability to trust others. To be successful, our managers had to communicate effectively with customers, employees, and the central office in Sioux Falls. Above all, our managers needed to have the discipline to start and finish any project required, while not losing track of the many extraneous details that were also part of the job.

We had tremendous success with our practice of hiring managers with liberal arts degrees in any field to run our equipment rental stores. This is an idea that is even more relevant now. In today's high tech business environment, especially "throughout the major U.S. tech hubs - whether Silicon Valley or Seattle, Boston or Austin, Texas - software companies are discovering that liberal arts thinking makes them stronger. Engineers may still command the biggest salaries, but . . . the war for talent has moved to nontechnical jobs, particularly sales and marketing." There is a real need to staff companies with "social alchemists who can connect with customers – and make progress seem pleasant." ("The Revenge of the Philosophy Majors", *Forbes,* August 17, 2015)

While we worked hard on incentives for every person in the business, we used formulas for the managers' pay that, in effect, made them partners. They also took half their bonuses after tax and bought stock in the company. Ownership was a strong work incentive, and managers, on average, owned 10 percent of their stores. They could climb a mountain or dig a hole with the freedom allowed under the management system. For comprehensive management of all aspects of their respective businesses, managers earned a nominal monthly base pay, and a bonus of up to 25% of before-tax profits. They had the option of investing their bonus and becoming active stockholders in their own operation. If stock in the other companies was available, managers could invest and become passive stockholders. When the firm was at a profitable level of operation, an assistant manager could be hired and paid for with 5% of the bonus. The theory was that sharing in the risks and rewards of their businesses inspired managers to go that extra step.

Lloyd, Bob, and Jim on 40th Anniversary of Elmen Rent All, 1990

While the umbrella organization - with guidance from major stockholders - maintained the right to hire and fire, and to set company-wide policy, each manager had a great deal of operational independence and was accountable for the profits and losses of his store. Aggregate monthly and annual reports generated by the central office provided data that helped managers see where their efforts and results fit into the bigger picture. They could see how each store compared with each other store, and with the average of the total operation. We held annual group manager meetings to discuss challenges and new policies or procedures. The meetings gave managers a chance to network and learn from each other. One of my ongoing challenges was to provide enough communication and support while also allowing managers to be as autonomous as possible. There always seemed to be a fine line between too much and too little communication, and I worked hard to determine where that line was for each manager. Part of my role was nudging them to bring out the best in themselves.

Carl Thompson was a Biology major at Augustana College, Sioux Falls. When he graduated in 1973 he came to work with us, and managed the Mason City, Iowa, store until 1999 when we sold the business. Carl told me recently that he remembers sitting in my office in the front of the old 12th Street location in June of 1973, on the day he was hired. He specifically remembers me saying, "I'm a millionaire, and someday I'm going to take a lot of people with me". Sometime in the late 1970s, Carl sent me an article he found in *Newsweek's* Business Forum about employee stock ownership plans (ESOPs) – at that time a relatively new vehicle for selling a business. We later had the occasion to discuss the subject as a potential vehicle going forward.

In the mid-1980s, my brother and I started to feel squeezed by the tremendous amount of cash required to support the continued expansion of rental stores in a growing number of states. There were also property expansions to finance, in addition to some new rental ventures - specifically, self-storage and rent-to-own appliance operations. A series of leadership meetings took place for the purpose of discussing ways to address the cash-flow problem. The two main ideas entertained were an initial public offering (IPO) and an employee stock ownership plan (ESOP) - the concept Carl Thompson and I had previously talked about. We had a lot of things going for us, but could we continue to be profitable with our headquarters in the sparsely populated and somewhat isolated state of South Dakota? If we didn't go public, and started an ESOP instead, would the world pass us by while our company stock grew and we ended up owing millions to our employees?

We were spending more and more cash on individual store expansions, and were still adding new properties to the rental store chain. Expanding throughout the region meant traveling longer distances from our company headquarters in Sioux Falls, South Dakota. Sharing a single-engine Beechcraft Bonanza plane with two other businesses seemed like a good way to visit the various stores, but we eventually went back to surface travel because our stores were not always close to airports.

To infuse the much-needed cash into our business, we ultimately decided to implement an employee stock ownership plan (ESOP). This solution had the added advantage of serving as a benefit and incentive for our employees. A significant part of a manager's pay depended upon individual store performance, and, because managers were stockholders in the company, it was in their best interest to work toward making the company as successful as possible. Our managers already owned 17.9 percent of our company. With the addition of another 22.55 percent, the ESOP brought the percentage to approximately 50 percent employee ownership over a seven-year period. Stockholders were also rewarded by a management system with high performing entrepreneurs in each store.

According to the National Center for Employee Ownership (NCEO), ESOPs were scarce until 1974, but by 2014 had been implemented by over 7,000 companies, impacting 13.5 million employees. Setting up an ESOP today typically costs upwards of $40,000, but once established, company contributions to the trust are tax-deductible, within certain limits. In an ESOP, a company sets up a trust fund, into which it contributes new shares of its own stock, or cash to buy existing shares. Shares in the trust are allocated to individual employee accounts.

As a private company, we were required to have an annual external valuation to determine the price of our shares. When employees left the company they received their stock, which we were required to buy back from them at fair market value. The future repurchase liability was thought of as the price paid for success, as well as a "thank you" to our employees. Employee stock ownership plans offer some attractive tax advantages and employee incentives, but to be truly effective, they should be combined with opportunities for employees to participate in decisions affecting their work.

The Elmen Rent All Inc. Employee Stock Ownership Plan and Trust was in existence from 1987 until 1999, when we sold our rental stores to United Rentals, Inc. I think it's fair to say that, not only did the ESOP enhance the financial well being of our employees when the company sold; it helped pave the way for an effective exit strategy for Elmen Rent All.

CHAPTER 14

Exit Strategy – Selling to a Publicly Traded Company

—ɱ—

Time is more valuable than money. You can get more money,

But, you cannot get more time.

~ JIM ROHN (1930-2009), AMERICAN ENTREPRENEUR & AUTHOR

A LONG-TERM BUSINESS STRATEGY SHOULD include an exit plan for the owners and perhaps for the business itself. In reality, an exit plan will - and probably should - evolve somewhat throughout the life of the company. Implementing an exit plan may be prompted by a need or a decision to pass the torch to someone else, a desire to dissolve the company, or an opportunity to sell the business. For us, a series of events and opportunities resulted in a chance to sell our rental store chain to United Rentals, Inc. (URI).

In 1997, a jet chartered by United Rentals landed in Sioux Falls with an acquisition team to discuss the purchase of our rental store chain. We refused their offer at that time - in part, because we had not reached our potential gross and profits. Because large companies typically trade at higher multiples, the market rewards the work of building a large business through the acquisition of smaller companies, which are often valued at lower multiples of earnings.

A successful rollup may involve acquiring smaller companies at, for example, 5 times EBITDA (earnings before interest, taxes, depreciation, and amortization), integrate them, and then sell the combined business for 7 times EBITDA. It is important that the consolidator be a strong company with some amount of critical mass that can get the process rolling.

United Rentals (URI) began trading on the New York Stock Exchange (NYSE) in 1997, the same year it began rental operations by acquiring six established equipment rental companies. By 1998, URI became the largest equipment rental company in North America when it bought U.S. Rentals, Inc. It continued its growth strategy and intensified its acquisition of companies (including ours) throughout 1999. It is now the largest equipment rental company in the world, with locations in 49 states and 10 Canadian provinces. The company's rental fleet (original equipment value of approximately $3 billion) consists of more than 500,000 individual units of rental equipment.

Before URI began trading on the New York Stock Exchange, CEO Bradley S. Jacobs and his acquisition team built up United Waste Systems, Inc. by purchasing more than 200 landfills and waste haulers. United Waste had shown that roll-ups (by which a company grows through continuing acquisitions) were a viable way of capitalizing on an investment. (United Waste Systems, Inc. was sold to USA Waste Services, Inc. in 1997, and United Rentals Inc. was formed.) It turned out that United Waste's acquisition and operating strategy was applicable to another industry. According to Silvia Sansoni in the June 1, 1998 issue of *Forbes* magazine, "Jacobs enlisted Merrill Lynch to help screen for new opportunities. Equipment rentals popped up and turned out to be a consolidator's dream."

Equipment rental was a booming business, where economies of scale were a tremendous advantage. For instance, larger rental companies could obtain 40 percent discounts on equipment that retailed for $50,000 or more. "One factor that favored the growth of the rental business was that contractors lost a deduction on purchased equipment when the tax code was changed in 1986. Then, the recession of the early 1990s forced many contractors to sell under-utilized equipment. Suitable acquisitions were tough to find because there was little public record of family-owned rental companies. So Jacobs read five years' worth of trade magazines, downloaded the web sites of hundreds of rent-al stores, and hired a private investigating firm with dozens of data bases to identify potential targets" (*Investors' Business Daily*, July 6, 1998).

United Rentals had quickly positioned itself to benefit from a general trend toward corporate outsourcing. Construction companies and other leading in-dustrial companies, municipalities, government agencies, and utilities recog-nized the advantages of renting equipment rather than incurring the expense of ownership. They discovered that renting offered many advantages: namely, avoidance of the large capital investment needed for purchasing equipment; access to a broad range of equipment for selecting the specific equipment best suited for each job; reduction of maintenance and storage costs; and the opportunity of renting the latest technology without having to pay for new equipment. 'What's driving this business day in and day out is that companies and individuals are discovering the benefits of renting over buying (fundin-guniverse.com).

United Rentals Inc. started buying smaller companies and gradually began to seek out the best companies, regardless of their size. By the end of 1998, we were fairly certain that Elmen Rent All had reached the point at which selling out would make sense. Early in 1999, URI visited us again with part of their acquisition team, and on July 1, 1999, we accepted their offer. I purposely planned a fishing trip in Canada that July with my son-in-law, Ken Gruys, and two of my grandkids - Hanna and Peter Elmen-Gruys. I wanted my attorney and accountant to handle the whole affair; if I was around they couldn't play good cop/bad cop.

In late 1999 United Rentals had completed the acquisition of our 47 rental store locations. In total, the URI had acquired 101 companies during the fiscal year, and had posted revenues of $2.23 billion, representing an 83 percent increase compared to the previous year. The U.S. equipment rental industry grew from about $600 million in annual revenues in 1982 to over $25 billion in 2000, an increase representing a compound annual growth rate of approximately 15 percent, according to United Rentals' data.

United Rentals Acquires Elmen and Udelson

Aug 1, 1999, Rental Equipment Register Staff

GREENWICH, Conn. "United Rentals has added two major players to its 550-plus location network, acquiring Elmen Enterprises, No. 14 on the RER 100, and Udelson Equipment, No. 30. United also completed its previously announced acquisition of Raytheon subsidiary Arayco, No. 38. Elmen brings 47 locations to United, which acquired the Midwest general equipment giant from senior management and employees, who owned 51 percent of the company via an employee stock option plan. The sellers were represented by M&A specialist Brown Brothers Harriman, New York. United is expected to use Elmen, which had $50 million in 1998 rental volume, as a platform to expand throughout the upper Midwest . . ."

Dad, with Jimmy (right) and me, 1939

Nearly fifty years after my father, Lloyd V. Elmen, began Elmen Rent-All by sending for a brochure in the mail and renting his personal property to the residents of Sioux Falls, South Dakota, we had closed the loop and sold the business. Dad would have been so pleased to see that his efforts so long ago had culminated in a successful sale to a publicly traded company.

CHAPTER 15

The Lasting Value of a Private Family Foundation

—⟋⟍—

What we have done for ourselves alone dies with us.
What we have done for others and the world remains and is immortal.

~ ALBERT PIKE (1809-1891), AMERICAN ENTREPRENEUR AND
BUSINESS PHILOSOPHER

AS A YOUNG MAN I did what most people did about taxes. I filled in the forms, figured the taxes due, and mailed everything in. Simple math and English skills were sufficient to do the job, and the tax preparation process was relatively straightforward and intuitive. Fast forward several decades to the current state of affairs, where the tax codes have become so complicated and change so often that many individuals, and virtually all businesses, have come to rely on professional tax preparers to stay up-to-date on tax laws and complete the myriad forms for submittal to the IRS. Even Albert Einstein, the brilliant physicist, seemed to agree when he said, "The hardest thing in the world to understand is the income tax."

Most people who have made a fortune (large or small) during their lifetime would agree that exercising a measure of control over what happens to that wealth after death is important. Our family is fortunate to have received consistently top-notch legal counsel over the years regarding estate-planning matters. There are many estate-planning tools that – depending on individual circumstances - may be effective in protecting family wealth from the lengthy, cumbersome, and inefficient probate process that whittles away what can be passed to future generations. One such tool is the Family Legacy Trust, which can provide a substantial benefit for heirs, particularly through the use of cash-rich life insurance. After funding the Legacy Trust with annual gifts, it can purchase insurance payable to your heirs, as beneficiaries of the Legacy Trust. The children and/or grandchildren would then receive a lump sum when you pass away. The proceeds from a Family Legacy Trust are typically 100% estate tax- and income tax-free, if structured properly.

The establishment of a private family foundation is another estate-planning tool – one that not only makes smart money sense, but also offers the opportunity to make a lasting impact on your local, regional, national, or even international community. In many cases, a foundation is an effective method for organizing your whole giving program, lifetime and beyond. Your family foundation can be a vehicle to teach children and grandchildren about leaving the world a better place, and can also bring family members together under a shared mission or purpose. In addition to instilling in children the significance of giving and compassion for those less privileged, a family foundation can curb a sense of entitlement that may come along with inheriting wealth.

Most family foundations are run by family members who serve on a voluntary basis as trustees or directors. Although auditors look for red flags that a family member is using funds as a personal piggy bank, a family foundation can provide employment for family members under certain circumstances. If your Foundation is earning 10% annually on its assets, but only paying 5% annually to charities, the difference can be distributed for legitimate expenses, including salaries for the directors of the Foundation, who may be family members. Salaries must be earned, with enough documentation to show that work was actually performed (Family Foundations Let Affluent Leave a Legacy, Kerry Hannon, *New York Times*, February 10, 2014).

I started looking more seriously at setting up a family foundation after reading about them in the writings of management guru Peter Drucker. To learn
more, I attended a national seminar in Chicago hosted by the Association of
Small Foundations (ASF). Two of our daughters, Julie and Sarah, have attended
various ASF (now Exponent Philanthropy) meetings in order to stay up to date
on various aspects of family foundations - such as creating an effective mission
statement; governance, tax, and legal issues; grant making principles; evaluat-
ing philanthropic impact; and legacy planning.

My younger brother Jim and I set up the Elmen Family Foundation together in
September of 1994. He and I had been partners in virtually all business ventures, and had shared everything from vehicles to vacation homes throughout
the years. We decided in 2006 that it would be better to create separate family
foundations so that, going forward, our respective families could make charitable giving decisions in accordance with their own goals and values. Jim passed
away on March 12, 2006 after a brave battle with Multiple Systems Atrophy,
an autoimmune disorder. He was always hardworking, a catalyst for getting
things done, and brought abundant energy to all of our shared ventures. He
loved his family dearly - wife Eloise, son Richard, daughters Connie Renee and
Rebecca - and doted on his grandchildren. Jim was an avid cyclist, and even
continued cycling during the decline of his health with the help of his son,
Richard, and a bicycle adapted for his use. To honor Jim's memory, the Elmen
Family Foundation established a bike station point with amenities for cyclists
along the Sioux Falls city bike trail.

Your last name doesn't have to be Gates, MacArthur, or Ford in order to create
a private foundation that makes a meaningful philanthropic impact. While up-
front legal costs can be somewhat prohibitive for smaller estates, sixty percent
of family foundations have assets of less than $1 million ("Family Foundations
Let Affluent Leave a Legacy", *New York Times,* February 10, 2014, by Kerry
Hannon). Running even a small family foundation can be a full-time job - and it
is for many. We try to make things as simple as possible, while also adhering to
the many rules governing the administration of a private foundation. We have

significantly minimized the administrative effort required to run our family foundation by not considering unsolicited grant requests. Instead, we identify nonprofits that align with our goals and ask them to submit a grant proposal. About half of our gifts are anonymous, in part, to save time.

In an effort to streamline the grant-making process for all parties, we try not to have a heavy hand regarding information requirements. Up to now, our application process has involved completing paper and pencil forms. We will undoubtedly streamline the process further by allowing nonprofits to submit their application online. I have dragged my feet somewhat on having a foundation web site, but my daughters are set on moving me forward in that direction. My initial concern was that an online presence would make us a target of unwanted attention and never-ending donation requests. This worry has been alleviated somewhat by the realization that we will be able to share our foundation's vision and goals, and clearly state the parameters of our grant-making process (for example, no unsolicited grant requests).

Private foundation founders must familiarize themselves with the myriad tax and other regulations involved. A foundation must be legitimate, like a real business. Books and records must be kept to show how decisions were made, and strict rules prohibiting self-dealing must be established. Grant-making foundations are subject to excise taxes for failure to make annual mandatory qualifying distributions of at least 5% of the value of the preceding year's average investment assets. All grant recipients must have a 501(c)(3) designation from the IRS. A foundation's grant making is public information; the 990 tax form can be viewed by anyone via the GuideStar. org web site.

Any appreciated assets transferred to your foundation can be sold by the foundation with no capital gains taxes. This is because of the foundation's charitable status. Every dollar contributed to your private family foundation means one less dollar included in your estate, and your contributions do not affect the current (2015) $14,000 annual gift exclusion or the $5.43 million lifetime gift exclusion. Under the current private foundation rules, a tax deduction of up to 30% of adjusted gross income for cash, and up to 20% for appreciated property, may be taken. Any income tax deduction not used in the contribution year may be carried forward over the next five years.

In recent years, we have been restructuring our philanthropic giving program to maximize long-term impact, primarily in the state of South Dakota. We select our grant recipients based on their proven potential for long, successful runs. And we generally refrain from funding operating expenses - preferring instead to support programming efforts and capital improvements. A few of our favorite philanthropic causes have included:

1) *The Augustana College Athletic & Event Center, Library, and Science Center*
   All of these grant recipients are on the campus of my undergraduate alma mater in Sioux Falls, South Dakota.

2) *The Center for Western Studies*
   The Center's mission is "improving the quality of social and cultural life in the Northern Plains . . . ". In addition to many other activities, the Center curates collections of art by Harvey Dunn and Oscar Howe, two South Dakota artists whose work Rita and I have enjoyed collecting.

3) *Good Earth State Park at Blood Run*
   Blood Run, a national historic landmark just southeast of Sioux Falls, SD, is one of the oldest sites of long-term human habitation in the United States; it was an important gathering place for seasonal ceremonies and a significant trading center for many tribal peoples from 1300 - 1700 A.D.

4) *Sioux Falls Area Community Foundation*
   Community Foundations, which serve charitable interests in a specific geographic area, are the fastest growing sector of U.S. philanthropy. We have prospered in the Sioux Falls community, and want to give back to our city.

Elmen family portrait commemorating our 60th wedding anniversary, 2012
(Back row: Peter Elmen-Gruys, Nick Setrakian, Michael Ackermann, Kjerstin
Elmen-Gruys Ackermann; Third row: Chris Ordal, Ken Gruys, Hanna Elmen-Gruys
Setrakian; Second row: Alex Kopp, Emily Ordal, Bob Kopp, Julie Elmen Gruys;
Front row: Sadie Kopp, Julia Kopp, Sarah Elmen Kopp, Rita Elmen, Bob Elmen;
not pictured: Brenda Elmen Ordal, Dan Ordal, Erik Ordal, Emily Marie Ordal)

Little did I know, when filling out those tax forms as a much younger man, how complicated life would get. I also had no way of foreseeing the fortuitous events or the bumps in the road that have made life so interesting and meaningful. You can count your "fortunes" in many ways - lessons learned, obstacles overcome, goals achieved, money made, or something else entirely. I am tremendously grateful for my fortunes.

Fifteen fortunes . . . and counting.

NOTES

www.ingramcontent.com/pod-product-compliance
Lightning Source LLC
Chambersburg PA
CBHW051321170526
45166CB00002B/638